The Targeted Evaluation Process

*A Performance Consultant's Guide to
Asking the Right Questions and
Getting the Results You Trust*

Wendy L. Combs and
Salvatore V. Falletta

ASTD

*Linking People,
Learning & Performance*

Ordering information: Books published by the American Society for Training & Development can be ordered by calling 800.628.2783 or 703.683.8100, or via the Website at www.astd.org.

Library of Congress Catalog Card Number: 00-104276
ISBN: 1-56286-140-9

CONTENTS

PREFACE

Evaluation has become one of the most challenging issues facing performance consultants today. An exciting transition from training to human performance improvement (HPI) is occurring, and performance consultants now have a broader range of HPI interventions at their disposal. Despite the proliferation of tools available to performance consultants for solving performance problems in the workplace, little has been done to advance evaluation practice beyond its current state.

The irony lies in the fact that evaluation leads to the thing held most dear by management: results it can trust. Evaluation is the process by which an organization can determine which interventions work and which ones do not. Evaluation helps the organization decide which interventions to weed out, discern areas for improving interventions, and—most important—justify expanding a successful intervention to other areas. Did performance improve? Was it sustained over time? What was its overall impact on the organization? These questions and many more are addressed by a process-driven approach to evaluation.

Despite its significance to the organization, evaluation is often overlooked or skipped in the interest of time. Too frequently, those responsible for HPI are pressured to abandon the evaluation process and embark on other, unrelated projects. The necessary statistical analysis may seem daunting. Just choosing from the plethora of evaluation tools can be overwhelming. This book can help performance consultants deal with these issues and more. Here we introduce a more flexible, meaningful approach for evaluating the quality, value, and effectiveness of HPI interventions via the six-step *targeted evaluation process,* which

- identifies stakeholders early in the evaluation process and gathers appropriate information that will yield data that meets the needs of all stakeholders—executives and senior managers seeking bottom-line results, line managers trying to improve workplace performance, and others
- warns of potential barriers to gathering meaningful evaluation results and indicates ways to eliminate those barriers

- allows the evaluator to consider evaluation dimensions, such as the usability of a job aid or the quality of the instructional design, when evaluating an intervention through a set of highly targeted questions
- guides the evaluator to select the right surveys, interview techniques, assessments, and other tools that will address the targeted evaluation questions
- helps the evaluator who is managing the evaluation process
- shows the evaluator how to communicate the results of the evaluation to all stakeholders.

The TEP process will be helpful to several different audiences, including

- performance consultants
- performance technologists
- HRD professionals
- instructional designers
- performance and needs analysts
- training specialists
- HR generalists
- OD practitioners
- managers who are accountable for HPI
- external consultants who specialize in HPI and evaluation.

This book is divided into three parts. Part 1 introduces evaluation within the context of the HPI process, describes the targeted evaluation process (TEP), and lists the skills and competencies required for carrying out the TEP. Chapter 1 includes an overview of HPI and introduces a variety of HPI interventions at our disposal. This chapter also calls for a new, targeted, process-oriented approach to evaluation, rather than the traditional, outcome-oriented models of evaluation. Chapter 2 describes the TEP in detail. Chapter 3 identifies the three primary roles that the performance consultant plays, with a focus on the role of the performance evaluator. The competencies required to carry out each step of the TEP are identified. A practical self-assessment tool and development plan is presented to aid the performance consultant in building these competencies through a variety of formal and informal means.

Part 2 first describes several popular HPI interventions—training, on-the-job training (OJT), job aids, electronic performance support systems (EPSSs), reward and incentive systems, and process improvement interventions. Chapter 8 covers two additional interventions that will likely become widely used in the near future, namely telework and knowledge management. This part of the book is organized so that readers may focus on those chapters and interventions that are most relevant to their current practice. The chapters identify useful evaluation questions and *evaluation dimensions*— specific factors, such as variables, processes, and outcomes, to consider when evaluating each type of intervention. Performance evaluators can adapt and build upon these questions and evaluation dimensions to tailor them to their own organization.

The last part of the book, part 3, is a how-to guide for conducting an evaluation. We have included this part of the book primarily for those who have not received formal training in research and evaluation methodology. Experienced performance evaluators may consider this section a review or optional reading. Chapter 9 presents the evaluation tools, technology, and techniques that are available with an emphasis on selection and design. Chapter 10 explains how to gather and analyze evaluation information, and Chapter 11 explains how to effectively report and present the evaluation results. Chapter 12 applies a project management framework to the TEP, and chapter 13 wraps up with questions that you may encounter as you bring TEP home to your organization.

This ambitious undertaking was supported by many people. We thank our mentors for their teaching and guidance. In particular, we would like to acknowledge Lisa Farwell, Bill Williams, Gail Hicks, Bill Barber, Tom Pyle, and Lee Swedberg at Eastern Washington University; Manindra Mohapatra, Samory Rashid, and Enamul Choudhury at Indiana State University; Bettye MacPhail Wilcox, Mike Ward, Bob Serow, Jim Burrow, George Baker III, and the faculty and staff in the department of adult and community-college education at North Carolina State University.

Several other people also played instrumental roles in the preparation of this book. Special thanks to Jim Pepitone, chairman and CEO of Pepitone Berkshire Piaget Worldwide, and Toni Hodges, measurement and evaluation manager at Bell Atlantic's department of training, education, and development, for their constructive feedback and suggestions.

Thanks also to our families and friends who were patient and supportive while we were writing this book: R.J. Combs, Suzanne Combs, Hope and Salvatore Falletta, Betty McGivern, Giovanna and Joseph Falletta, Grace Wright, Brandon Falletta, Logan Falletta, Michelle Combs, Jennifer Combs, Ilene Combs Blanco, Cesar Blanco, Joe Falletta, Chris Davis, Donna and Steven Peterson, Mike Falletta, Eric Falletta, John Lavering, Chris Marsh, Mike Russell, Dan DeMarte, Michael Lovelace, Christie and Scott Mabry, Elizabeth Feild-Pisculli, and Jill Murphy-Lamb.

Finally, we acknowledge each other's contributions not only to this book, but to the many activities involved with defending two dissertations, relocating to the West Coast, and surviving the heights of Mount Whitney (14,497 feet).

Wendy L. Combs
Salvatore V. Falletta
October 2000

PART 1

EVALUATION: CLOSING THE HPI LOOP

EVALUATION: WHY BOTHER?

"Acceptable evidence about performance must rely on measurement. If science does nothing else, it measures, and we must become very good at measuring human performance. As a general rule, our clients in the workplace are not good at it, and here is where we can be of especially great help. We can have our greatest effects on human performance just by measuring performance correctly and making information available" (Gilbert, 1992).

Strategic Questions Answered

Why are organizations increasingly moving toward a performance orientation?

What is human performance improvement?

How are the many HPI interventions categorized?

What are the fundamental steps of the HPI process?

Where does evaluation fit into the HPI process?

How does the TEP relate to human performance improvement?

To maintain a competitive advantage in today's global economy, organizations are continually searching for opportunities to increase workplace performance and productivity. Organizations, however, have become more strategic and cost conscious in their choice of business solutions. Increasingly, they are demanding customized solutions that take into account their unique business needs. A systematic process is available for analyzing performance problems and designing or customizing solutions and interventions. This process is human performance improvement (HPI).

Human Performance Improvement in a Nutshell

Human performance improvement is a relatively new field that is grounded in several broad theoretical domains such as economic theory, psychological theory, and systems theory (Swanson, 1999). The field has also been strongly influenced by other applied disciplines and practices, including behavioral psychology, instructional systems design and development, ergonomics and human factors, scientific management, psychometrics, human resources, industrial and organizational psychology, human learning processes, and the cognitive sciences (Stolovitch and Keeps, 1992; Dean and Ripley, 1997; Kaufman, Thiagarajan, and MacGillis, 1997).

Human performance improvement is "a systemic and systematic approach to identifying the barriers that prevent people from achieving top performance" (Sugrue and Fuller, 1999), to solving performance problems, and to improving opportunities in the workplace. The term is generally synonymous with human performance technology (HPT), which Robinson and Robinson (1998) define as "the science of improving human performance in the workplace through analysis and the design, selection, and implementation of appropriate interventions." Unfortunately, neither definition explicitly states that measurement and evaluation are included in the HPI process; yet, they are essential to the field and practice of HPI (Bates, 1999; Holton, 1999).

The HPI process involves five fundamental steps (figure 1-1):

- performance analysis
- root-cause analysis

4

- intervention selection and design
- implementation
- evaluation.

Performance Analysis

The first step of the HPI process is performance analysis. The purpose of performance analysis is to understand and validate the nature of the perceived performance problem. During this step, performance consultants gather information on the symptoms and frequency of the problem, its relative importance, and the value in solving the problem. A detailed assessment of the problem is carried out through various methods, including interviews with employees and observation of workplace activities and outputs to document the current state of performance. This analysis may be relatively simple or complex depending on the scope of the perceived performance problem. A description of the desired state of performance is then constructed and validated with stakeholders. The difference between these two states represents the performance gap to be resolved.

Instructional designers and training professionals sometimes refer to performance analysis as front-end analysis or needs assessment. Although there are differences in these types of analyses, front-end analysis and needs assessment are rooted in instructional systems design and are predisposed toward instructional interventions. Performance analysis is not predisposed toward the use of one intervention over another in closing the performance gap.

Root-Cause Analysis

The next step of the HPI process, one that is often overlooked, is root-cause analysis. Root-cause analysis identifies those factors that cause or contribute to the performance problem. Rosenberg (1996) contends that the underlying

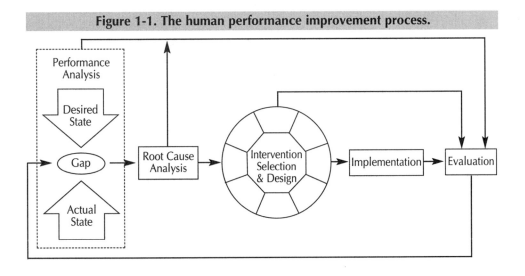

Figure 1-1. The human performance improvement process.

causes of performance problems are typically attributable to one or more of the following:

- a lack of data, information, or consistent feedback
- a lack of environmental support, resources, or tools
- a lack of consequences, incentives, or rewards
- skills, knowledge, and attitudes
- motivation and expectations
- individual capacity.

If the root cause of the problem is not identified, the intervention may address only symptoms of the underlying problem. The likelihood of selecting and designing an effective intervention is much greater if a proper root-cause analysis has been carried out.

Intervention Selection and Design
Once the performance and root-cause analysis have been validated with stakeholders, the intervention is selected and designed. To portray the variety of solutions that are available, an intervention wheel is depicted in figure 1-1. Because such a broad spectrum of interventions is available to the performance consultant, it is important to select the most appropriate intervention. When selecting an intervention or combination of interventions, the performance consultant must consider several factors:

- nature and scope of the problem
- underlying causes
- cost and available resources
- time required for the design and implementation of the solution
- probability that the solution will close the performance gap.

Various types of HPI interventions are available to the performance consultant (Dean and Ripley 1997, 1998a,b,c). Because no universally accepted typology of HPI interventions is available, we have categorized interventions into two broad areas: instructional and noninstructional (table 1-1).

Instructional interventions are designed to promote knowledge and skill acquisition or attitude change through instructor-led training, small group activities and workshops, and training through other media (for example, computer-based training, video-based instruction, and distance learning). Training aids may be used in conjunction with instructional interventions; they provide additional information to support classroom learning. Self-paced instruction is another instructional intervention that enables the employee to learn at his or her own pace without the aid of an instructor. In addition, structured on-the-job training (OJT) is designed to facilitate knowledge and skill mastery in the work environment instead of in the classroom.

The noninstructional category of interventions includes a broader range of performance interventions. One of the simplest, yet effective, noninstruc-

Table 1-1. A sampling of HPI interventions.

Instructional Interventions	Noninstructional Interventions
Instructor-led training	Elimination of barriers
Small group activities and workshops	Job aids
Computer-based training	Electronic performance support
Video-based instruction	systems
Self-paced instruction	Feedback systems
Distance learning	Performance expectations
Training aids	Coaching and mentoring programs
On-the-job training	Job design or redesign
	Process design and improvement
	Organization design or redesign
	Personnel selection
	Incentive systems
	Telework
	Knowledge management
	Cultural change initiatives
	Organization development

tional solutions involves the identification and elimination of barriers to performance in the work environment. Another noninstructional intervention is the job aid. The job aid is similar to the training aid, except that job aids are used on the job, precisely when they are needed. Job aids provide information, prompt procedures, or make answers readily available as a reference for the employee (Rossett and Gautier-Downes, 1991). Electronic performance support systems (EPSSs) are similar to job aids; however, they are computer-based integrated systems that provide employees with online help and expert advice.

Noninstructional interventions that involve guidance from managers to improve performance include feedback systems, performance expectations, and coaching and mentoring programs. A feedback system may be a formal or informal means to provide feedback about job performance to an employee. Managers may also establish performance expectations as part of the performance appraisal system. In addition, coaching and mentoring programs enable less experienced employees to increase their skill and competence on the job. Coaching may be used for feedback or as part of a corrective action process to encourage or reinforce desirable behaviors and discourage undesirable behaviors within the context of work.

Also under the category of noninstructional interventions are those involving the design or redesign of jobs, processes, or organizations. Job design is the process of creating or redesigning jobs so that they are more enriching and meaningful to workers. The goal of job design is to increase worker motivation and performance. On the other hand, process redesign involves simplifying business processes and procedures to increase organizational effectiveness and efficiency. At a higher level, organizational redesign involves establishing new strategies, structures, and systems to enhance the overall functioning of the organization.

Large-scale initiatives in the noninstructional category of interventions include personnel selection, incentive systems, culture change initiatives, organization development, and knowledge management. Personnel selection involves selecting "the right person for the right job" to minimize performance problems in the future. Once the individual is employed, incentive systems are designed to motivate or influence workers to perform by providing monetary (performance bonuses, stock options, and so forth) and nonmonetary (career opportunities, for example) rewards and recognition. At the organizational level, culture change initiatives are aimed at changing the underlying values, beliefs, and norms that guide individual and team behavior. Organization development, which is a field of practice in and of itself, involves numerous strategies for improving inter- and intragroup relationships within the organization. Finally, knowledge management is the process of creating, capturing, and using the collective knowledge—the intellectual capital—within an organization.

Implementation

The next step of the HPI process is implementation. Whether implementing a small- or large-scale initiative, it is critical to manage the implementation or rollout of the intervention over the duration of the project (Fuller, 1997). Some of the critical success factors associated with successful implementation are project sponsorship, adequate resources, a communication and change management strategy, and alignment of related initiatives.

Evaluation

Evaluation is the last step of the HPI process. Evaluation is the systematic process of gathering and analyzing data and other objective information on HPI processes and outcomes within the context of the business or organizational setting to determine the quality, value, and effectiveness of the intervention or solution. The term *systematic* emphasizes the series of steps involved in planning and conducting the evaluation of an HPI intervention.

Although organizations often skip evaluation in the interest of time, it is a critical activity in the ongoing cycle of improving performance in the workplace. Without evaluating the quality, value, and effectiveness of interventions, there is no way to know whether the intervention was successful. Moreover, without evaluation, stakeholders cannot gauge the success of the intervention. Some other reasons for evaluation are to

- determine whether the intervention was implemented as designed
- assess if the goals and objectives of the intervention were met
- decide whether to continue, leverage, or terminate an intervention
- determine if the intervention was the most appropriate or best solution
- predict if the improved performance is sustainable over time

- provide information for decision making and business planning
- demonstrate the value of the HPI process in general
- build commitment and support for future interventions or initiatives
- promote collaboration and organizational learning (lessons learned).

Traditional Evaluation Frameworks: Misconceptions and Shortcomings

Evaluation is supposed to close the loop of the HPI process model, but, unfortunately, this final step of the HPI process sometimes is considered "optional" and is skipped or overlooked! If an evaluation is carried out, often it is performed in a perfunctory manner. This laissez-faire attitude toward evaluation can be attributed to the widespread popularity and adoption of traditional evaluation frameworks, such as Kirkpatrick's four-level model of training evaluation (Kirkpatrick, 1998), which was designed for evaluating training and not other HPI interventions. Moreover, it fails to consider critical intervening variables, factors, and processes related to the success of an intervention (Holton, 1996; Bernthal, 1995).

Kirkpatrick's seminal model was introduced in 1959 (Kirkpatrick, 1998) and has been used extensively ever since, even warranting a mention in the *Human Resources Kit for Dummies* (Messmer, 1999). The four levels of this model are described in table 1-2.

The first level involves measuring learners' reactions (their satisfaction) to training. Learning as a result of training is measured at level 2, and performance (the learners' behavioral changes) is measured at level 3. The fourth level of Kirkpatrick's model refers to the final results of training; this last level is measured with production, quality, and cost metrics. Each of the levels in the model is entirely outcome-oriented.

A number of variants of Kirkpatick's model have emerged, including the addition of a "fifth" level to reflect training's ultimate value (Hamblin, 1974), societal value (Kaufman and Keller, 1994), and return-on-investment (Phillips, 1997). Despite these attempts to improve or build upon Kirkpatrick's and other traditional models, they still fall short. In fact, some (Holton, 1996; Tesoro and Tootson, 2000) say these should not be called models because they are merely taxonomies (predetermined lists) of training outcomes.

Table 1-2. Kirkpatrick's four-level model for evaluating training.

Level 1 (reaction)	Participants' reaction to training
Level 2 (learning)	Participants' change in attitude, knowledge, or increase in skill
Level 3 (behavior)	Participants' behavioral change
Level 4 (results)	Final results that occurred as a result of participants' participation in the program

Several misconceptions are associated with Kirkpatrick's model. The most common ones are the following:

- *Misconception 1:* Training can be adequately evaluated by measuring the levels or outcomes of the model.
- *Misconception 2:* The lower levels of the model must be measured before the upper levels are.
- *Misconception 3:* A causal relationship or linkage exists among the levels.
- *Misconception 4:* The upper levels of the model are superior to the lower levels.
- *Misconception 5:* The level of the model dictates which evaluation method and which tool will be used.
- *Misconception 6:* The model is applicable to any HPI intervention including noninstructional interventions.

The first misconception arises because training cannot be completely evaluated by the model, because it does not include any process measures—only outcome measures. Hence, many intervening factors that can affect the success of training are not considered. The second misconception arises because the upper levels of the model can be measured independently. The levels can be measured in any order. In fact, research has shown that the lower levels of the model are not dependent on the upper levels, nor are the levels causally related to each other (Alliger and Janak, 1989). The fourth misconception crops up because measuring outcomes from the upper level of the model is not inherently better than measuring outcomes from the lower levels. Rather, the most valid measure is the one that answers the targeted evaluation question posed by the stakeholders.

The fifth misconception has generated much debate. It concerns the use of a specific evaluation tool with each level of the model. Many practitioners and academicians believe that the level dictates which tool should be used. For example, level 1 requires surveying, level 2 requires testing, and so on. In reality, there are many different ways to measure the same thing, and some of these tools are more valid than others. Rather than using a predetermined tool, the performance evaluator and stakeholder must consider the questions to be answered and the appropriate evaluation dimensions. Armed with that information, they can then agree on an evaluation tool. The final misconception concerns the applicability of Kirkpatrick's training evaluation model to HPI interventions. Kirkpatrick's model, or taxonomy, was designed for instructional interventions, such as training, yet it is frequently and inappropriately applied to noninstructional HPI interventions.

A more flexible and meaningful approach for evaluating HPI interventions is sorely needed. As this book's title *The Targeted Evaluation Process: A Performance Consultant's Guide to Asking the Right Questions and Getting the Results You Trust* suggests, it is our goal to provide a better way to evaluate the quality, value, and effectiveness of HPI interventions.

The Targeted Evaluation Process

The targeted evaluation process (TEP) is a process approach to evaluation. The TEP has several features that distinguish it from traditional evaluation frameworks such as the Kirkpatrick four-level model (table 1-3).

Table 1-3. Comparing the TEP and Kirkpatrick's four-level evaluation model.

Targeted Evaluation Process	Kirkpatrick's Four Levels
A flexible and meaningful approach to evaluation	A limited, simple approach to evaluation
A six-step process of evaluation that is stakeholder-driven	A taxonomy or listing of outcomes that is predetermined
Applicable to a wide range of interventions	Limited to instructional interventions such as training
Considers the organizational context in which the intervention is embedded	Considers the intervention in isolation
Focuses on targeting evaluation questions and identifying evaluation dimensions with stakeholders	Focuses on the levels
Uses the full range of evaluation tools, technology, and techniques that are available	Uses a few tools that are dictated by the level
Accounts for intervening factors and processes that may affect the success of the intervention	Does not account for intervening factors and processes
Evaluates the quality, value, and effectiveness of an intervention	Evaluates the outcomes of an intervention only
Is vital to the overall HPI process	Is considered an optional and perfunctory activity

The TEP is a flexible and meaningful approach to evaluation that involves a six-step process of:

1. partnering with stakeholders
2. understanding the intervention and organizational context
3. targeting evaluation questions and identifying evaluation dimensions
4. designing tools, technology, and techniques
5. gathering and analyzing data
6. reporting results.

The first three steps of the TEP provide meaningful and acceptable evidence of the quality, value, and effectiveness of an intervention. The final three steps of the TEP represent the mechanics of evaluation. These six steps represent a process-oriented approach to evaluating a broad range of

HPI interventions. Special emphasis is placed on partnering with stakeholders; understanding the intervention and the organizational context in which it is embedded; and targeting evaluation questions and identifying evaluation dimensions that are relevant to a particular intervention. The TEP is vital to the ongoing cycle of improving performance in the workplace, and, most important, the TEP provides results that performance evaluators and stakeholders can trust.

WHAT IS THE TARGETED EVALUATION PROCESS?

"The dominant evaluation model, the four-level Kirkpatrick model, has received alarmingly little research and is seldom fully implemented in organizations . . . Reliance on the simple four-level taxonomy, and particularly on reactions as an outcome, only serves to minimize the value, impact and sophistication of the intervention tools HRD employs and the results that can be achieved" (Holton, 1996).

Strategic Questions Answered

Why is a new approach to evaluation sorely needed?

What are the distinguishing features of the targeted evaluation process?

What are targeted evaluation questions and evaluation dimensions?

How do you carry out the six-step targeted evaluation process?

How do you assess the organizational context of an intervention?

How do you identify and involve stakeholders in the TEP?

What is involved in project-managing the TEP?

In a recent study by the Conference Board, a global business membership organization dedicated to improving business enterprises, 315 training and HR executives from large companies, including IBM, USAA, Motorola, and 3M, were surveyed (Hackett, 1997). In considering the value of interventions, such as training, executives were clearly dissatisfied with current evaluation practices, including Kirkpatrick's model and return-on-investment (ROI) analysis. They criticized the Kirkpatrick model for its lack of applicability to a wide range of HPI interventions and the omission of many important intervening factors that enable or inhibit performance. They also thought the calculation of ROI was inappropriate for many interventions because value is not easily quantified in dollar amounts and too many estimates and assumptions are required. In their call for a new and better way to evaluate interventions, they recommended an approach that

- is flexible enough to measure the wide variety of interventions in use today
- takes into account the many variables and factors that enable and inhibit performance
- focuses on both the processes and outcomes of interventions
- provides information for decision making
- ensures stakeholder return-on-expectations (ROE).

The Targeted Evaluation Process

The TEP is a systematic approach for evaluating a broad range of HPI interventions. As distinct from traditional evaluation approaches, the TEP involves partnering with stakeholders, understanding the intervention and the organizational context in which it is embedded, targeting evaluation questions, and identifying evaluation dimensions that are relevant to a specific intervention. This approach takes into account the relevant factors (intervening variables and so forth), processes, and outcomes associated with the intervention being evaluated. The six steps of the TEP are presented in table 2-1.

Step 1: Partnering with Stakeholders
Partnering with stakeholders is an ongoing process of establishing and building rapport, credibility, and trust. According to Robinson and Robinson

Table 2-1. The targeted evaluation process.

Step 1: Partnering with stakeholders

Step 2: Understanding the intervention and organizational context

Step 3: Targeting evaluation questions and identifying evaluation dimensions

Step 4: Designing the tools, technology, and techniques

Step 5: Gathering and analyzing data

Step 6: Reporting results

(1998), performance consultants spend at least 25 percent of their time cultivating relationships with stakeholders and sponsors. This partnership between performance consultants and stakeholders is fundamental to improving performance and central to the TEP. Partnering with stakeholders is important to

- secure commitment, involvement, and support of the evaluation
- identify informational needs, expectations, and priorities
- provide communication on the ongoing progress of the evaluation
- increase ownership of the results, both positive and negative
- ensure utilization of the evaluation recommendations.

Who are the stakeholders? A stakeholder is anyone who is directly or indirectly affected by an HPI intervention or evaluation. Stakeholders include executives (business owners or sponsors), senior managers, line managers, employees, and, in some cases, customers, suppliers, vendors, and contractors. Each stakeholder has a different perspective and set of concerns regarding the intervention and evaluation; these informational needs are captured in table 2-2.

Whereas managers are usually most interested in the implementation process (how smoothly the implementation of the intervention is going), senior managers and executives are usually more interested in how the intervention affects the business. Line managers prefer detailed information for managing the implementation, whereas senior managers prefer aggregate information for comparing business units. On the other hand, executives prefer high-level summaries of bottom-line results to support strategic planning and decision making. The type of information that is important to stakeholders should be identified early in the evaluation process.

Step 2: Understanding the Intervention and Organizational Context
It is essential to gain an intimate understanding of the nature of the intervention or combined interventions being evaluated. This is accomplished by gathering and reviewing all information related to the intervention, for example, collaborating with team members, and accessing other relevant sources of information (best practices in the field, benchmarking data, and so forth).

Table 2-2. Gauging stakeholders' informational needs.

Process Focus ◄──────────────────────────► Results Focus		
Line managers are interested in:	**Senior managers are interested in:**	**Executives are interested in:**
• what is happening with the intervention • implementing the solution to achieve objectives • descriptive information to guide implementation • detailed, unabridged information	• whether the solution was appropriate • the accomplishment of short-term goals • the analysis of patterns and trends • aggregate information on the performance of business units or departments • variations from the expected results	• the impact of the intervention on the business • the accomplishment of longer-term organizational goals • a synthesis of information for implications • highly aggregated information • exception reporting to quickly identify problems and opportunities

The critical elements of the intervention that should be fully understood at this step of the TEP include:

- the purpose of the intervention
- the intervention goals and objectives
- the size and scope of the intervention
- the expected results.

Depending on the complexity of the intervention, a visual graphic or model of the major inputs, processes, and outputs may be created to better understand the nature of the intervention. The intervention should also be described in terms of the organizational context in which it is embedded.

The organizational context is important to consider during the TEP because factors in the larger organization may account for its success or failure. Performing evaluation in isolation without considering the organizational system in which it operates is likely to yield results that cannot be fully interpreted. The most important contextual factors in the organization to consider include

- organizational values, mission, and strategy
- business performance goals and objectives
- organizational culture
- political climate
- business policies, processes, and procedures
- communication channels
- human and fiscal resources
- problem history.

These factors should be informally or formally assessed in relation to the intervention. The purpose in doing so is to identify potential barriers and problems in advance, to plan a meaningful evaluation, and later, to facilitate the interpretation of the results that are gathered and analyzed. Strategies for assessing these factors are presented in table 2-3.

This assessment is ideally performed up front as part of the root-cause analysis step of the HPI process. In practice, however, it is rarely adequately

Table 2-3. Assessing the organizational context.

Factor	Assessment Strategy
Organizational values, mission, and strategy	Describe how the HPI intervention does or does not align with the organization's values, mission, and strategy.
Business performance goals and objectives	Describe business performance goals and objectives.
	Anticipate the impact of the intervention on current goals and objectives.
Organizational culture	Describe the organizational culture.
	Assess the organization's readiness for change.
	Describe the behavior that is informally rewarded.
Political climate	Identify influencers and powerful stakeholders who are directly and indirectly involved in the intervention or evaluation.
Business policies, processes, and procedures	Describe current business policies, processes, and procedures that relate to the intervention.
	Anticipate the impact of the intervention on existing policies, processes, and procedures.
Communication channels	Describe how communication typically flows through the organization both formally and informally.
	Identify the most commonly used communication vehicles.
Human and fiscal resources	Identify trends in human and fiscal resources (e.g., cyclical patterns, budgetary constraints, employee turnover).
	Identify the human and financial resources required to support the intervention through design, pilot-testing, implementation, and maintenance.
Problem history	Describe previous change efforts within the organization and business unit (successes, failures, lessons learned).
	Describe current related interventions or initiatives.

carried out. It is important to analyze the organizational context early in the TEP. Furthermore, if any significant organizational changes occur (organizational restructuring, introduction of new technology, change in leadership, and so forth), these contextual factors should be revisited.

Step 3: Targeting Evaluation Questions and Identifying Evaluation Dimensions

Once the intervention and the organizational context are understood, the next step is to generate targeted evaluation questions. Since stakeholders tend to pose broad evaluation questions based upon their experience or curiosity, the performance evaluator should facilitate working sessions with stakeholders to replace these broad questions with targeted evaluation questions. The process of targeting evaluation questions and identifying evaluation dimensions involves conducting working sessions with stakeholders. The performance consultant or evaluator should prepare in advance for these sessions to ensure that the sessions are focused and productive (figure 2-1).

Targeted evaluation questions are specific, focused questions that lend themselves to measurement. Table 2-4 shows examples of both broad and targeted evaluation questions for two HPI interventions.

The question "Does the job aid increase the user's performance?" is broad and calls for a simple yes or no. In contrast, the corresponding targeted evaluation questions are more specific and measurable. These questions are much more useful because they elicit detailed information. Targeted eval-

---

Figure 2-1. To-do list for stakeholder working sessions.

Prior to the session:
- Identify stakeholders.
- Gather existing information on the intervention.
- Secure location, room, equipment, and materials.
- Prepare an agenda with the objectives to be accomplished.
- Prepare a high-level overview of the intervention.

During the session:
- Present the overview of the intervention.
- Discuss stakeholder informational needs.
- Brainstorm evaluation questions.
- Categorize questions by theme.
- Identify the evaluation dimensions that are represented in the themes (use part 2 of this book to identify additional relevant dimensions).
- Prioritize evaluation dimensions.
- Wrap up the session.

After the session:
- Consider holding additional working sessions as needed.
- Generate targeted evaluation questions from the prioritized list of evaluation dimensions.
- Hold another session to validate and achieve consensus on the targeted evaluation questions and evaluation dimensions.

Table 2-4. Examples of evaluation questions.

Noninstructional Intervention	
Broad Evaluation Question	**Targeted Evaluation Questions**
• Does the job aid increase the user's performance?	• To what extent have employees' error rates decreased? • To what extent has employees' speed in troubleshooting customer problems increased? • To what extent has the number of orders processed each day increased?
Instructional Intervention	
Broad Evaluation Question	**Targeted Evaluation Questions**
• Can the instructional design of the training be improved?	• Are the learning objectives of the training clear, specific, and measurable? • To what extent does the instructional design provide for practice and feedback to ensure mastery of the learning objectives? • To what extent does the instructional design define learner training preparation before, during, and following training?

uation questions can even be so specific that they automatically lend themselves to measurement with a specific tool. At this step of the TEP, however, discussions about the use of a particular evaluation tool, technology, or technique would be premature and limiting.

By targeting evaluation questions, the performance evaluator can identify evaluation dimensions to include in an evaluation. Evaluation dimensions are relevant factors, processes, or outcomes associated with an intervention. There are numerous evaluation dimensions to consider in any particular evaluation. For example, the evaluation dimensions that may be addressed in the evaluation of a job aid include the usability of the job aid, error reduction due to use of the job aid, and maintenance of the job aid, among others. Evaluation dimensions that may be of interest when evaluating training include instructional design, learning, and transfer climate, to name a few. Examples of evaluation dimensions related to training, OJT, job aids, EPSS, rewards and incentives, process improvement, telework, and knowledge management are presented in part 2 of this book. The purpose of identifying evaluation dimensions is to focus the evaluation on desired outcomes (expected results) and relevant intervening variables that are important to stakeholders. In short, evaluation dimensions bring issues of importance into sharper focus. The evaluation dimensions presented in this book are drawn from theory, research, and practice. Some are relevant to all HPI interventions (stakeholder satisfaction and performance), whereas others are unique to a particular intervention. In either case, the listing of evaluation dimensions in this book is not meant to be exhaustive.

The process of targeting evaluation questions and identifying evaluation dimensions is iterative because questions stimulate dimensions and vice versa (figure 2-2). Thus, the performance evaluator may wish to include additional targeted evaluation questions after identifying evaluation dimensions. Multiple targeted evaluation questions are required to adequately address a given evaluation dimension. Usually several different evaluation dimensions are included in an evaluation.

Step 4: Designing the Tools, Technology, and Techniques

During the next step of the TEP, the performance evaluator selects and designs the tools, technology, and techniques to be used in the evaluation to address the targeted evaluation questions and evaluation dimensions that stakeholders have identified. The performance evaluator can select from several different types of evaluation tools: surveys, interviews, focus groups, observations, assessments, and key business metrics (customer value, quality, efficiency, and so forth).

These tools can be designed in new technological formats to aid data gathering and analysis. Examples of this technology include: email, fax, diskette, CD-ROM, scannable technology, Web-based technology, and interactive voice response (automated telephone polling). In most cases, the performance evaluator must identify, construct, and customize the appropriate tools and technology. Chapter 9 includes a practical guide on how to select and design evaluation tools, use technology as appropriate, and apply specific techniques for gathering and analyzing evaluation data.

The decision about which tools, technology, and techniques to use should be driven by the targeted evaluation questions and evaluation dimensions that are identified and stakeholders' perceptions of the credibility of the tools, technology, and techniques. Stakeholders must believe in and agree with the

Figure 2-2. The iterative cycle of targeting questions and identifying dimensions.

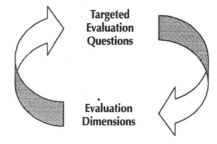

choice of tools, technology, and techniques that are to be used for the evaluation. If they do not, the evaluation results will not be viewed as credible. Stakeholder buy-in is essential.

Step 5: Gathering and Analyzing Data

This step of the TEP involves the actual collection of the evaluation data and statistical analysis and interpretation. Since evaluation data is ideally gathered from multiple sources (observations of performance, interviews, key business metrics, and so forth) at different points in time, the performance evaluator plays an important role in coordinating and monitoring data gathering.

The potential complexity of the evaluation highlights the need to project-manage the TEP. If technology is used, the coding and analysis of the data, or part of the data, may be automated. When the analysis is not automated, the performance evaluator plays an instrumental role in coding, analyzing, and interpreting the evaluation data. The statistics that the performance evaluator uses will depend on the level of data collected on the evaluation tools; the use of common statistics to evaluate HPI interventions is covered in chapter 10. These statistics enable the performance evaluator to describe, compare, and interpret the data in relation to the targeted evaluation questions and evaluation dimensions.

Step 6: Reporting Results

Communicating the results of the evaluation to stakeholders is a critical step of the TEP. It is the culmination of the evaluation: the information that stakeholders have been waiting for! Communicating the results serves many purposes, including

- answering the targeted evaluation questions for decision making and planning
- providing evidence of the quality, value, and effectiveness of the intervention
- stimulating important questions from stakeholders and their continued involvement
- marketing the intervention and the usefulness of the TEP in general
- documenting lessons learned in the organization.

It is very important that the evaluation results are directly linked to the targeted evaluation questions and the evaluation dimensions that were to be addressed by the TEP.

The evaluation report is one of many different vehicles for communicating the results and recommendations of the evaluation. Other communication vehicles are formal presentations, email notices, the company's intranet, and newsletters. Marketing vehicles, such as pamphlets, posters, and videos, are also frequently used for communication. The information should be customized for specific audiences. For instance, presentations are typically developed according to stakeholders' informational needs and expectations and the objectives of the communication. Useful suggestions on preparing an evaluation report and recommendations and developing a communication matrix for dissemination of the results are presented in chapter 11.

Project-Managing the TEP

Although the TEP involves only six steps, the evaluation process should be managed within a project-management framework. This approach ensures that evaluation activities and deliverables are completed on schedule and within budget. Usually, a project plan captures these activities and deliverables for resource allocation, dependency planning, risk analysis, and contingency planning. This project plan may roll up into an overall project plan for the entire HPI process. The evaluation activities that tend to consume the most time are:

- working sessions with stakeholders
- constructing and piloting evaluation tools
- training HPI staff
- procuring and setting up evaluation technology
- data gathering activities
- generating reports and other communication.

Examples of typical evaluation activities and deliverables associated with the TEP are presented in table 2-5, and chapter 12 is dedicated to project management of the TEP and the overall HPI process. Keeping the evaluation on track in terms of time and money is a vital part of closing the HPI loop and ensuring stakeholder satisfaction.

Table 2-5. A project-management framework for the TEP.

TEP Step	Activities and Deliverables
Step 1: Partnering with stakeholders	• Identify key stakeholders (e.g., business owners, clients) of the HPI intervention and evaluation and their informational needs, expectations, and priorities. • Explain the TEP and secure commitment and support. • Plan working sessions and communication with stakeholders.
Step 2: Understanding the intervention and organizational context	• Review the original analysis and design documents related to the intervention. • Interview program designers and interventionists on the history and background of the intervention. • Assess the organizational context of the HPI intervention.
Step 3: Targeting evaluation questions and identifying evaluation dimensions	• Conduct working sessions to target evaluation questions and identify evaluation dimensions. • Agree on the scope and goals of the evaluation with stakeholders. • Agree on major evaluation activities, deliverables, and timeline. • Identify, acquire, and assign resources. • Contract for evaluation activities.
Step 4: Designing the tools, technology, and techniques	• Construct evaluation tools (e.g., observation forms, assessments, surveys). • Pilot evaluation tools, check reliability and validity, make necessary revisions. • Procure and set up technology (e.g., optical scanning, database) as appropriate. • Identify participants, determine sampling strategies, participating locations, timing, and logistics. • Plan the evaluation design, including the timing of tool administration, dates, and length of time required. • Train HPI staff in tool administration.
Step 5: Gathering and analyzing data	• Collect relevant business metrics over time. • Supervise or monitor data collection and verify data quality. • Use technology for tool administration and data coding, analysis, and reporting to the extent possible. • Code data from each evaluation tool if not automated. • Perform statistical analysis. • Prepare tables, charts, and so forth. • Interpret compiled data in relation to the targeted evaluation questions and evaluation dimensions.
Step 6: Reporting results	• Clarify ongoing reporting requirements. • Generate recommendations (e.g., improvements) for the intervention. • Write evaluation report. • Prepare communication plan. • Design presentation package(s). • Obtain stakeholders' feedback on evaluation documents and make necessary revisions. • Conduct meta-evaluation (i.e., postmortem) and document lessons learned.

NEW REQUIREMENTS FOR THE PERFORMANCE EVALUATOR

*"In the 1980s, the job of the performance con-
sultant did not exist. This job was created in the
early 1990s in a few organizations that required
a role that partnered with line management
and had a strong focus on performance
improvement . . . Now, in the late 1990s, performance consultant is a job title in numerous
organizations and is certainly a role in others"*
(Robinson and Robinson, 1999).

Strategic Questions Answered

What are the three primary roles of the
performance consultant?

What are the competencies associated with the performance evaluator role?

Which of these competencies do you, as a performance evaluator, need to develop?

How can you develop these competencies?

T his chapter focuses on requirements for the performance consultant who takes on the new role of performance evaluator. The competencies related to this critical role of evaluator are described in relation to each step of the TEP. To aid the performance evaluator with developing these competencies, a self-assessment tool and development plan are presented.

The Many Roles of the Performance Consultant

The job of the performance consultant has been widely discussed in the HPI literature. For example, performance consultants come from a variety of professional backgrounds, including HR, OD, line management, engineering, and training, and can assume a variety of specialized roles (developer, intervention specialist, subject matter expert, and so forth). Indeed, performance consultants represent an eclectic mix of practitioners with unique sets of experiences, skills, characteristics, and values. They also vary in their level of expertise with specific HPI interventions. Performance consultants usually perform three main roles: performance analyst, project manager, and performance evaluator (figure 3-1).

It is widely agreed that the performance consultant fills the role of performance analyst, and there is increasing realization of the importance of the performance consultant's role in project-managing the HPI process (Fuller, 1997). Little has been said, however, about the role of the performance consultant as an evaluator. This chapter focuses on the competencies that are required of the performance evaluator.

Figure 3-1. The three "hats" of a performance consultant.

Performance Analyst Project Manager Performance Evaluator

The Competencies of the Performance Evaluator

The performance consultant who is serving as performance evaluator must possess certain competencies (table 3-1).

In step 1 of the TEP, consultation skills and knowledge of the business are essential to building credibility and trust with stakeholders. Once a partnership is established, the performance evaluator attempts to make sense of the intervention and organizational context through assessment and diagnosis as part of step 2. To do so, the performance evaluator should have a basic understanding of the intervention and an in-depth understanding of organizational culture and behavior. During step 3, the performance evaluator assists stakeholders in targeting evaluation questions and identifying evaluation dimensions to include in the evaluation. This requires strong group facilitation skills and the ability to build consensus with a potentially large and diverse group of stakeholders.

Steps 4, 5, and 6 require more technical evaluation competencies to carry out the mechanics of the TEP. For example, to design the tools to be used in the evaluation, the performance evaluator should have a solid background in constructing surveys, tests, and instruments. Observation, questioning, and interviewing skills are also required for gathering data. Familiarity with available technology is particularly useful when gathering large amounts of data. For example, the performance evaluator may recommend the purchase of a specific technology to facilitate ongoing data collection, analysis, or reporting.

The ability to analyze and interpret evaluation data is a required competency in step 5. This includes statistical analysis and interpretation of data in some cases. Although technology is available to automatically calculate simple statistics, the performance evaluator should have a conceptual understanding of the statistical methods being used, as well as their underlying assumptions and limitations. Furthermore, when interpreting trends in key business metrics, the performance consultant should be confident in judging the practical significance of data in terms of the results and statistical variations.

The most visible step in the TEP is the performance evaluator's ability to effectively communicate and report evaluation results. The performance evaluator must be able to persuasively package the evaluation results. The performance evaluator should be able to recommend strategies for communicating and marketing the results and implementing change to improve performance.

Not every organization has a professional evaluator with all of these competencies. Performance consultants can develop these competencies; they can also rely upon each other to augment their own skills. In fact, it is a good idea to encourage performance consultants to focus on developing different competencies so that they can work together as a team.

A self-assessment of the competencies required of the performance evaluator is presented in figure 3-2.

Table 3-1. Required competencies of the performance evaluator.

Step 1: Partnering with Stakeholders	Step 2: Understanding the Intervention and Organizational Context	Step 3: Targeting Evaluation Questions and Identifying Evaluation Dimensions	Step 4: Designing the Tools, Technology, and Techniques	Step 5: Gathering and Analyzing Data	Step 6: Reporting Results
Consultation skills	Business knowledge and perspective	Group facilitation skills	Observation skills	Supervising and monitoring skills	Effective presentation skills
Business knowledge and perspective	Familiar with HPI interventions	Effective listening and communication	Questioning and interviewing skills	Statistical analysis skills	Marketing skills
Knowledge of the HPI process	Political awareness	Questioning and interviewing skills	Survey, test, and instrument construction	Organization and interpretation of information and data	Political awareness
Responsive to stakeholders' needs and expectations	Understanding of organizational culture and behavior	Problem-solving skills	Knowledge of key business metrics	Ethical decision making, judgment, and integrity	Influence and persuasion
Building credibility and trust	Assessment and diagnostic skills	Building consensus	Research and evaluation design		Change management and adaptability
	Systems thinking		Familiarity with available technology		

Project management skills are necessary for all steps of the TEP.

Figure 3-2. Self-assessment for competencies of the performance evaluator.

Directions: Rate the extent to which you have mastered each of the following competencies by circling a number from 1–7. After you have completed all items, highlight the competencies that fall within the lower range (i.e., 1–3). Identify a few competencies (no more than five) that are high priorities for your development. Transfer these development priorities to your performance evaluator development plan.

	Not at all					To a great extent		Development Priority — Low	Development Priority — High
1. Assessment and diagnosis skills	1	2	3	4	5	6	7		
2. Building consensus	1	2	3	4	5	6	7		
3. Building credibility and trust	1	2	3	4	5	6	7		
4. Business knowledge and perspective	1	2	3	4	5	6	7		
5. Change management and adaptability	1	2	3	4	5	6	7		
6. Consultation skills	1	2	3	4	5	6	7		
7. Effective listening and communication	1	2	3	4	5	6	7		
8. Effective presentation skills	1	2	3	4	5	6	7		
9. Ethical decision making, judgment, and integrity	1	2	3	4	5	6	7		
10. Familiar with available technology	1	2	3	4	5	6	7		
11. Familiar with HPI interventions	1	2	3	4	5	6	7		
12. Group facilitation skills	1	2	3	4	5	6	7		
13. Influence and persuasion	1	2	3	4	5	6	7		
14. Knowledge of key business metrics	1	2	3	4	5	6	7		
15. Knowledge of the HPI process	1	2	3	4	5	6	7		
16. Marketing skills	1	2	3	4	5	6	7		
17. Observation skills	1	2	3	4	5	6	7		
18. Organization and interpretation of information and data	1	2	3	4	5	6	7		
19. Political awareness	1	2	3	4	5	6	7		
20. Problem-solving skills	1	2	3	4	5	6	7		
21. Project-management skills	1	2	3	4	5	6	7		
22. Questioning and interviewing skills	1	2	3	4	5	6	7		
23. Research and evaluation design	1	2	3	4	5	6	7		
24. Responsive to stakeholders' needs and expectations	1	2	3	4	5	6	7		
25. Statistical analysis skills	1	2	3	4	5	6	7		
26. Supervision and monitoring skills	1	2	3	4	5	6	7		
27. Survey, test, and instrument construction	1	2	3	4	5	6	7		
28. Systems thinking	1	2	3	4	5	6	7		
29. Understanding of organizational culture and behavior	1	2	3	4	5	6	7		

This self-assessment is for your own personal use and development. Complete the self-assessment honestly and objectively, relying upon your past learning and work experiences. After you have rated yourself on each of the competencies, identify a few as priorities for development. Use the performance evaluator development plan (figure 3-3) to create a strategy for developing or strengthening each area you have identified.

Building Your Competencies

Many strategies are available for developing the competencies of the performance evaluator. Some formal strategies are

- enrolling in graduate programs and courses at universities and colleges
- attending institutes, workshops, and seminars offered by professional organizations
- participating in certificate programs
- joining national and local professional associations and attending those conferences.

Informal strategies for developing specific competencies include

- mentoring and coaching relationships
- information exchange though lessons learned and knowledge sharing
- networking with other performance consultants
- actively working on HPI projects
- self-directed reading of recommended books and journals
- Internet resources.

The Additional Resources section of this book lists a number of recommended readings and Internet resources dedicated to HPI and evaluation.

Figure 3-3. Performance evaluator development plan.

The competency I plan to develop	My current level of performance	Development strategy	Anticipated completion date	Success indicator

PART 2:

APPLYING THE TEP

Training and On-The-Job Training

"Training is the process through which skills are developed, information in provided, and attitudes are nurtured, in order to help individuals who work in organizations to become more effective and efficient in their work. Training helps the organization to fulfill its purpose and goals, while contributing to the overall development of workers . . ." (Davis and Davis, 1998).

Strategic Questions Answered

Why are organizations predisposed toward the use of training as an HPI intervention?

What are some of the barriers to the effective transfer of learning to the work environment?

When is structured OJT the most appropriate HPI solution?

What are the benefits of structured OJT?

Which evaluation dimensions are appropriate for evaluating training and structured OJT?

Part 2 of this book is dedicated to specific HPI interventions. In these chapters, you will learn why:

- Training is a *legitimate* solution (contrary to popular belief).
- On-the-job training is a *practical* solution.
- Job aids are *cheap* solutions.
- EPSS is an *integrated* solution.
- Reward and incentive systems are *SMART* solutions.
- Process improvement is a *neglected* solution.
- Telework and knowledge management are *emerging* solutions.

Since the purpose of these chapters is to illustrate the use of TEP, each chapter suggests targeted evaluation questions and evaluation dimensions for each of the interventions. These examples can be used as an excellent starting point for step 3 of the TEP. Then the performance evaluator and the stakeholders can tailor the targeted evaluation questions and evaluation dimensions to their own organizations.

This chapter provides an overview of training and OJT and suggests some targeted evaluation questions and evaluation dimensions related to these two interventions. The information provided would be most helpful to performance evaluators who are involved in the evaluation of training or OJT. Many of the ideas about training and OJT will be familiar to the performance consultant, although some concepts are new or rarely associated with evaluation. The concepts presented here provide a basis for defining evaluation dimensions, which are discussed later in the chapter.

Training

Training is an instructional intervention familiar to performance consultants. The different types of training activities that occur in organizations today include executive and leadership development; managerial and supervisory development; technical skills training; computer skills training; sales and marketing training; customer service training; workplace safety and health training; and basic workplace skills training. Many methods are used to deliver employee training; the most widely used method is leader- or instructor-led training in the classroom. Other media used for training delivery are video-based instruction, computer-based training, intranet and Internet-based training, and distance learning. Another form of training that occurs in the work environment is OJT. The evaluation of OJT is presented in the latter part of this chapter.

A Legitimate Solution

Organizations today rely extensively on training as the primary approach to HPI. Although there is a call within the field to move "beyond training to performance" (Robinson and Robinson, 1995, 1998), the use of training to solve performance problems is likely to continue. Because the notion of training is deeply embedded in the history and culture of organizations, it is the first solution that comes to mind when a performance problem arises. Performance consultants should not be predisposed toward any one type of HPI solution, but they should consider training to be a legitimate solution, among others, for addressing performance problems.

Targeting Evaluation Questions

The identification of targeted evaluation questions enables the performance evaluator and evaluation team to identify the relevant evaluation dimensions for evaluating training. The targeted evaluation questions address different facets of training. For example, some questions (table 4-1) focus on instructional design, and others pertain to learner characteristics and the work environment. Additional targeted questions relate to training outcomes, such as job performance. Note that this table is not an exhaustive list of all possible targeted evaluation questions; it does, however, offer some examples to guide and inspire performance consultants who are engaged in the evaluation of training.

Targeted evaluation questions can be very specific. A particular evaluation tool may even come to mind when answering the questions. At this point however, the goal is to identify the targeted evaluation questions, rather than the particular methodology to be used. The technical aspects of the evaluation are planned after the targeted evaluation questions and evaluation dimensions are identified.

Evaluation Dimensions Related to Training

Targeting evaluation questions helps identify the evaluation dimensions to include in an evaluation and vice versa. Evaluation dimensions are relevant factors, processes, or outcomes associated with a particular type of intervention, in this case, training. The evaluation dimensions to consider in the evaluation of training are

action planning	prerequisites
competency	stakeholder satisfaction
instructional design	trainer effectiveness

Table 4-1. Examples of targeted evaluation questions related to training.

Instructional Design

- Were the characteristics of learners (i.e., the intended audience) identified prior to the design of the training? Did these characteristics (e.g., learning preferences) drive the design?
- Were the training objectives written in advance of the content development? Were they clear, specific, and measurable?
- To what extent did the instructional design provide for practice and feedback to ensure mastery of the learning and achievement of performance objectives?

Learner Characteristics

- Were learners interested in the content of the training?
- To what extent did learners perceive the training to be relevant to their jobs?
- To what extent were learners motivated to apply the newly acquired skills on the job?
- What mode of training delivery did learners (i.e., the intended audience) prefer?

Work Environment

- Did managers value the training? Did they communicate this value?
- Did learners have the opportunity to apply what was learned in training on the job? How much time did managers provide for learners to practice newly acquired skills?
- What were the consequences of performing the newly acquired skills? To what extent did learners receive positive reinforcement and feedback for applying the new skills?

Performance on the Job

- To what extent did learners' performance improve?
- Were there any unanticipated effects of the training on performance? Which factors enabled or inhibited learners' performance?
- To what extent did the training intervention close the performance gap?

learner characteristics	training delivery
learning	training environment
media effectiveness	training relevancy
organizational context	transfer climate
organizational results	transfer strategies
performance on the job	work environment.

Not all of these evaluation dimensions would be included in an evaluation; rather, the evaluation dimensions to be included in a given evaluation depend on stakeholder requirements and the targeted evaluation questions that are posed. Some evaluation dimensions are intuitive, but others are based on research and practice in training. Among the most important evaluation dimensions are instructional design and development, training delivery, transfer of training, learner characteristics, the work environment, the transfer climate, action planning, and competency modeling.

Instructional design and development of the training are important determinants of training effectiveness. To evaluate instructional design and development of a training intervention, the performance evaluator can interview designers and review the design document and training materials. If the design of the training appears to be sound—based on performance analysis—an evaluation of the training delivery may be warranted. To determine whether the training is being delivered as planned, the performance evaluator can observe training sessions to ensure that different trainers are delivering the training in the same way and that the trainers are adhering to the instructional design. The performance evaluator must bear in mind this caveat: Even with sound instructional design, development, and delivery as planned, the transfer of learning to the job is not assured.

The transfer of learning refers to the learners' application of the knowledge and skills they acquired in training to their job immediately following the training (Broad and Newstrom, 1992). Since the main goal of training is to increase performance, training transfer is critical. Training transfer depends on three major factors. The first factor concerns the characteristics of the learner (Berardinelli, Burrow, and Dillon-Jones, 1995; Newstrom and Lengnick-Hall, 1991; Baldwin and Ford, 1988). Table 4-2 lists some characteristics of the learner that may affect training transfer.

The purpose of identifying these learner characteristics is to highlight the potential for collecting evaluation data on the effectiveness of the training

Table 4-2. Characteristics of learners that may affect transfer of training to the job.

Absorption of the material
Attention span
Attitude toward the training
Commitment to the training
Dominant needs in relation to work (e.g., orientation toward achievement)
Expectations for the training
Interest in the training content
Level of skepticism
Personality (e.g., locus of control)
Motivation to learn
Perceptions of the practicality of the training
Perceptions of the relevance of the training to the job
Resistance to change
Self confidence in applying new skills

Newstrom and Lengnick-Hall, 1991; Baldwin and Ford, 1988

transfer. For example, if you find considerable variability in learners' on-the-job performance of the new skills, the differences in learner characteristics—rather than training design or delivery—may account for the variability. By including this particular evaluation dimension and collecting relevant data, the performance evaluator may collect useful information for interpreting training outcomes.

The second major factor to consider with respect to training transfer is the work environment in which learners attempt to apply their newly acquired skills. Some work environments are more supportive of employees' attempts to practice and apply the skills than are others. Factors in the work environment that can affect training transfer include

- opportunity and time to perform the skills
- consequences of performing the skills (positive reinforcement, negative reinforcement, punishment, lack of reinforcement, and so forth)
- managers' perceptions of the training and its effectiveness
- organizational culture and climate.

The characteristics of learners and the various factors within the work environment act in synergy to create a transfer climate that affects the transfer of learning to the job. In other words, if a learner does not have a positive attitude about performing the skills on the job and the work environment is not supportive, training transfer is very unlikely. Co-workers can also have an effect on training transfer. For example, co-workers may subtly influence the learner to resist change and maintain the status quo (Broad and Newstrom, 1992). Research is currently being conducted to discern the most important factors associated with the transfer climate in organizations; tools to measure transfer climate are also being constructed and tested (Holton et al., 1997; Rouiller and Goldstein, 1993). Figure 4-1 shows some examples of survey questions related to several evaluation dimensions for transfer of learning to the job.

Many strategies can enhance the transfer of learning to the job. These strategies pertain to manager, trainer, and learner behaviors before, during, and after training. The goal is to establish a triangular partnership of managers, trainers, and learners to support the learner as he or she applies the skills learned in training. Broad and Newstrom (1992) provide many suggestions for facilitating learning transfer.

Another factor, which may have a positive effect on training transfer, is action planning. This strategy involves planning the specific actions a learner intends to take to apply the newly acquired skills on the job (Youker, 1985). Action planning is sometimes referred to as performance contracting and may occur before, during, or after training. The purpose of action planning is to enable the learner to identify barriers to training transfer in an attempt to overcome these barriers. Since learners decide when, where, and how they will apply their new learning, they are essentially developing personal learning-

Figure 4-1. Examples of survey questions related to several evaluation dimensions for a particular job skill.*

Job Skill #1	Response Alternative
1. To what extent did the *training prepare* you to perform this skill?	Not at all To a great extent 1 --- 2 --- 3 --- 4 --- 5
2. To what extent is this skill *relevant* to your job?	Not at all To a great extent 1 --- 2 --- 3 --- 4 --- 5
3. To what extent have you had the *opportunity* to perform this skill on the job?	Not at all To a great extent 1 --- 2 --- 3 --- 4 --- 5
4. Did you *perform* this skill on the job?	☐ Yes ☐ No
5. To what extent are you *confident* in your ability to perform this skill?	Not at all To a great extent 1 --- 2 --- 3 --- 4 --- 5
6. To what extent are you *encouraged* to use this skill on the job?	Not at all To a great extent 1 --- 2 --- 3 --- 4 --- 5
7. Did you and your manager discuss *action planning* in relation to the training to help you apply the new skills you learned?	☐ Yes ☐ No

*These examples were drawn from a follow-up survey of learners who participated in a training intervention.

transfer plans. Some practitioners believe that all types of training should include suggestions and advice to the learner on how to apply learning after the learner returns to the work environment (Foxon, 1997; Youker, 1985).

Another important evaluation dimension for training is the notion of competency. Organizations have recently become interested in developing competency models to guide employee training and development efforts (Parry, 1998; McLagan, 1997; Mirabile, 1997). Although the use of competency models has increased, there is considerable misunderstanding as to what a "competency" is. People often use the term competency when they actually mean skill. Competencies are also confused with personality traits and values. According to Parry (1998), a competency is a cluster of related knowledge, attitudes, and skills that affect a major part of an employee's job. Cherniss and Adler (2000) go one step further. They define emotional competency as "a learned ability, based on emotional intelligence, that improves job performance. Emotional competencies can include attitudes and beliefs, as exemplified by achievement drive and self-confidence, as well as skills and abilities. Emotional competencies, however, are learned; they are not innate. People are not born with a high degree of self-confidence or achievement drive." Unlike personality traits or values, competencies affect job performance, employees differ in their level of proficiency with respect to competencies, and, most important, employees can enhance emotional competencies with the right interventions.

If a competency model has been constructed and validated within your organization, stakeholders may be interested in assessing the extent to which training is linked to the competencies in the model. Stakeholders will also want to know how effectively the training helps employees develop core competencies.

No single evaluation effort can address all of the evaluation dimensions of training. The performance evaluator should focus on the most meaningful and relevant evaluation dimensions based on the features of the intervention, the organizational context, and stakeholders' needs and expectations.

On-the-Job Training

On-the-job training is a form of training that occurs in the work setting itself. It can be either structured or unstructured (informal). In both types of OJT, a more experienced employee serves as a trainer in the development of other employees (Jacobs and Jones, 1995). The informal approach to OJT involves pairing two employees, enabling the less experienced employee to learn from the more experienced employee. In contrast, the structured approach to OJT involves analysis of the skills to be learned, formal design and development of learning activities, and selection and training of OJT trainers.

The use of OJT in the work setting ensures that employees learn how to perform tasks in accordance with the standards and expectations of the work group. This method is particularly useful in training new employees, and it can significantly reduce the time required for an employee to come up to speed in a new work environment. The immediate feedback a learner receives from the OJT trainer establishes and strengthens relationships between co-workers and increases learners' self-confidence in performing the newly acquired skills. With OJT, training transfer is not an issue because the skills are learned and practiced in the actual work setting, and the learner usually has ongoing access to the trainer for support and reinforcement.

A Practical Solution

As is the case with all HPI interventions, the use of OJT should be recommended as the solution to a performance problem only after sufficient performance and root-cause analyses have been performed. On-the-job training may be one of several different types of training that can be used to address the performance problem. In general, OJT is recommended when

- the skills to be learned need to be performed regularly
- the skills can only be acquired over time through practice
- only a few employees need to be trained at the same time
- the work environment is conducive to learning
- experienced employees are willing and able to serve as OJT trainers
- learners are motivated and can work with minimal supervision.

If the information to be learned will not be used regularly on the job or if the information frequently changes, OJT is probably not the best training alternative. Furthermore, if experienced employees are not willing or able to serve as trainers, OJT may not feasible. If OJT would disrupt normal work patterns or production schedules or if the work environment is noisy, busy, or stressful, OJT is probably not appropriate (Nolan, 1996).

Targeting Evaluation Questions

By identifying targeted evaluation questions, the performance evaluator and evaluation team can elucidate the relevant evaluation dimensions for evaluating OJT. Many examples of targeted evaluation questions for OJT, which may be relevant to your evaluation efforts, are presented in table 4-3.

Because OJT is an instructional intervention, many of the targeted evaluation questions are similar to those posed for training. Questions that are unique to OJT deal with the appropriateness of the learning tasks for OJT; the recruitment, selection, and training of OJT trainers; and the work environment in which the OJT is delivered.

Table 4-3. Examples of targeted evaluation questions related to OJT.

OJT Trainer Selection

- Were a formal process and criteria established for recruiting and selecting OJT trainers?
- What were the characteristics of employees who volunteered to be OJT trainers?
- Did an adequate pool of potential OJT trainers exist within the organization?

OJT Environment

- Was the work environment conducive to OJT?
- Were all of the necessary tools, equipment, and technology readily available and operable in the OJT environment?
- To what extent did managers allocate resources (e.g., people, time) to support the OJT program?

Certification

- Was the OJT linked to an internal certification process? To what extent were the OJT objectives and content aligned with the certification assessment tool or process?
- Were the criteria for performance clear, specific, and agreed upon by experts? To what extent did learners demonstrate this competence and consistent performance?
- Did customers believe the OJT is a critical component of the certification program?

Organizational Results

- How did the OJT program effect quality, productivity, and efficiency measures?
- To what extent was the OJT program addressing the identified performance gaps at the organizational level?
- How did the structured OJT program compare to alternative interventions (e.g., classroom training) in terms of effectiveness and cost?

Evaluation Dimensions Related to OJT

The process of targeting evaluation questions helps identify evaluation dimensions to include in an evaluation. The evaluation dimensions to consider in the evaluation of OJT are

certification	OJT trainer effectiveness
competency	OJT trainer selection
learner characteristics	organizational context
mentoring relationship	organizational results
OJT delivery	performance on the job
OJT design	prerequisites
OJT environment	stakeholder satisfaction
OJT learning	Train-the-OJT-Trainer.

Not all of these evaluation dimensions would be included in an evaluation; rather, the decision about which evaluation dimensions are included in a given evaluation depends on stakeholder requirements and the targeted evaluation questions.

Some of the most important factors related to OJT include the formal design and development of the learning activities; the recruitment, selection, and training of the OJT trainer; the OJT training environment; the mentoring relationship; and the potential to link certification efforts to OJT.

Is Training the Right Intervention?

Organizations often turn to training—whether in the classroom or on the job—as an HPI intervention because the notion of training is deeply embedded in the history and culture of organizations. Performance consultants should not be predisposed toward any one type of HPI intervention, but they should consider training to be a legitimate solution, among others, for addressing stakeholders' needs or correcting performance problems. By applying the six-step TEP process, you can gauge the quality, value, and effectiveness of training in your organizational setting.

5

JOB AIDS AND ELECTRONIC PERFORMANCE SUPPORT SYSTEMS

"Some experts claim that these items can work wonders. They save money. They save time. They save marriages. They enhance training. They replace training. They improve performance. And they do all of these things at reduced cost to the organization. What miracles are these that promise so much power at a fraction of the cost of other kinds of . . . interventions? The answer is job aids" (Rossett and Gautier-Downes, 1991).

Strategic Questions Answered

What are job aids and when should they be designed as an HPI solution?

In which paper-based and technological formats are job aids designed?

What is an electronic performance support system (EPSS) and what type of information does it contain?

When should an EPSS be designed to solve a performance problem?

Which evaluation dimensions should be considered in evaluating job aids and EPSSs?

This chapter provides an overview of job aids and EPSSs and suggests some targeted evaluation questions and evaluation dimensions related to these two interventions. Targeting evaluation questions and identifying evaluation dimensions are critical steps in the TEP. Many of the ideas and concepts about job aids and EPSSs will be familiar to the performance consultant although some may be new or rarely associated with evaluation. The concepts presented here provide a basis for the evaluation dimensions that are presented later in the chapter.

Job Aids

A job aid, or performance aid, is a tool used to support employees' performance. The job aid is typically a paper-based reference that contains information to guide and direct work activities on the job. The information on the job aid may prompt employees to perform certain procedures or make decisions when needed (Rossett and Gautier-Downes, 1991; Rossett, 1995). For example, a job aid can be developed to support a complex activity that is performed infrequently such as entering codes into a system (Harless, 1989). The use of the job aid in this case eliminates the need for employees to rely on their memory and thus reduces the likelihood of errors. Moreover, job aids can be used to standardize work procedures if there is considerable variability in employees' performance or if the consequences of errors are great (Reynolds, 1996). Because it is one of the least expensive HPI interventions to develop, the job aid is the most commonly used noninstructional HPI intervention.

The list of job aids is long: step-by-step checklists and worksheets, decision matrices and flowcharts, diagrams and illustrations, reference and procedural guides, and many more. Specific examples of job aids are

- small folding cards with telephone voicemail commands
- laminated posters displaying safety procedures
- an instruction sheet on how to set up and use a new Palm Pilot
- a worksheet for selecting employee benefits and calculating the costs of benefits to be deducted from pay

- listings of product and service codes for completing a purchase requisition
- a flowchart identifying each activity a sales associate must complete to process a customer order
- a label, which lists steps for turning on and using a piece of equipment, mounted on the tool.

Job aids can be printed in color, printed on cardstock, laminated, spiral-bound, or tented to stand up on desk tops. The size of the job aid can vary considerably. For example, paper-based job aids may be small (pocket-size), medium (for desktop display), or large (poster). With advances in technology, job aids may also be designed as part of an integrated EPSS.

When deciding whether to develop a job aid to support performance, the performance consultant must consider the characteristics of the intended users. For example, job aids are not appropriate if psychological factors prevent employees from using the job aid, for example, if the employee's credibility would be diminished because the customer expects a knowledgeable expert. Furthermore, if speed during performance is required, employees would not have time to pull out and read the job aid. Job aids can help standardize employees' performance by ensuring that performance is consistent. Nevertheless, because job aids cannot cover all scenarios that employees might encounter, job aids are not advisable for employees who frequently encounter novel or unpredictable situations. Furthermore, if the intended users lack basic reading and referencing skills, a job aid is probably not the most appropriate HPI solution. Several comprehensive references are available to help the performance consultant decide on appropriate formats and develop job aids (Harless, 1989; Rossett and Gautier-Downes, 1991).

A Cheap Solution

Using a job aid to solve a performance problem is one of several possible HPI solutions. Although training prepares learners to perform in the future, job aids are available where performers need them—on the job—and when they are needed—immediately. Compared to other HPI interventions, the job aid is less costly to develop and implement and can be quickly and easily updated. The performance consultant may choose job aids over other HPI solutions if time or resources are limited. Furthermore, job aids may be developed to support other HPI interventions such as training or EPSS. When job aids are developed and implemented in conjunction with training, they offer additional benefits:

- Job aids may reduce the length of training by supplementing or supplanting the training (Rossett and Gautier-Downes, 1991).
- Job aids may enhance the quality of training by emphasizing the relevance of the training to performance on the job.
- Job aids may facilitate the transfer of learning from the training classroom to the work environment.

Targeting Evaluation Questions

Identifying targeted evaluation questions enables the performance evaluator and evaluation team to identify the relevant evaluation dimensions for evaluating job aids. Table 5-1 presents many examples of targeted evaluation questions, some of which pertain to the development of the job aid, the accuracy and usability of the job aid, and the maintenance of the job aid. Some of these targeted evaluation questions can be used to improve the job aid while it is still in development. These examples of targeted evaluation questions may be relevant to your particular evaluation effort.

Evaluation Dimensions Related to Job Aids

The process of targeting evaluation questions serves to identify the evaluation dimensions to include in an evaluation and vice versa. Evaluation dimensions are relevant factors, processes, or outcomes associated with a particular type of intervention, in this case, job aids. The evaluation dimensions to consider when evaluating job aids are

accuracy	performance on the job
business process integration	standardization of procedures
error reduction	stakeholder satisfaction
implementation of the job aid	organizational results

Table 5-1. Examples of targeted evaluation questions related to job aids.

Job Aid Development

- Was the job aid designed based on user needs?
- Was the job aid pilot-tested with actual users before implementation?
- Is the wording on the job aid simple, clear, and consistent?
- Can the readability of the job aid be improved by using color coding, highlighting, white space, bullets, or outlining?

Accuracy

- Does the job aid contain all the critical information?
- Is the data in matrices and tables accurate?
- Are the steps on the job aid ordered correctly?

Usability

- Do employees find the job aid easy to use?
- Is it easier for employees to ask co-workers for help than to use the job aid?
- To what extent does the job aid answer employees' questions?
- What percentage of employees' time is spent using the job aid?

Job Aid Maintenance

- Is the job aid durable or must it be maintained or replaced often?
- Is the job aid maintained as needed (e.g., when changes and updates are required)?
- Is there a mechanism in place for notifying users of updates? For producing and distributing updates in a timely manner?

job aid development   up-to-date content
job aid maintenance   usability.
organizational context

Not all of these evaluation dimensions would be included in an evaluation; rather, the choice of which evaluation dimensions to include in a given
evaluation depends on stakeholder requirements and the targeted evaluation
questions. Some of the evaluation dimensions are self-evident. Several evaluation dimensions—the usability of the job aid, business process integration,
and job aid maintenance—are discussed in more depth here.

The usability of the job aid in supporting employee performance is one
of the most important evaluation dimensions to include in an evaluation of a
job aid. To be usable, the job aid must contain all of the needed information,
it must be accurate, it must be up-to-date, and it must be convenient.
Employees must be aware of the job aid's content, be able to understand the
information, be able to timely access the information, and successfully apply
the information on the job.

Depending on the type of job aid, it may be important to determine
whether the information on the job aid is integrated into business processes.
To avoid confusing employees, the content and steps on the job aid should
mirror the formal business processes within the organization. The job aid
must also be relevant to the intended users' roles and responsibilities or else
it will go unused. Usually this problem stems from insufficient performance
analysis before the job aid was designed.

The way in which the job aid is maintained is another evaluation dimension that may be relevant to an evaluation. More often than not, establishing
procedures to update the job aid is a neglected step in the development
process. The details associated with maintaining job aids include identifying
the individuals who will be responsible for the updates, determining the frequency of updates, planning frequent evaluations of the ongoing usefulness
of the job aid, and reporting the availability of the job aid to a central group
within the company for tracking purposes.

Electronic Performance Support Systems

Electronic performance support systems are computer-based systems that
provide a user with information, advice, or tools to support performance at
the moment of need (Gery, 1991). The information that is provided may be a
fact, a concept, an example, or a procedure. The EPSS may be a complex, integrated technological system that is implemented throughout the organization or a smaller tool that is implemented within a specific function. The EPSS
may have interfaces to several sources of information such as databases
already existing within the organization. Furthermore, an EPSS may provide
embedded (intrinsic) support to the user or linked (extrinsic) support as a

separate interface. With an intrinsic support tool, the user does not have to leave the task at hand to access the EPSS.

The different types of EPSSs include infobases, expert systems, help systems, interactive productivity software, monitoring systems, and feedback systems. The term infobase, coined by Gery (1991), refers to an electronic knowledge base or database that contains relevant information employees need to perform their jobs. For example, employees regularly need to access product information and specifications, schematics, diagrams, business policies, and procedures. These infobases are stored and organized in hypertext tools, online documentation software, text retrieval software, and database management systems. The most effective infobases are comprehensive, logically structured, and appropriate to users' task requirements (Gery, 1991). Figure 5-1 lists several different EPSSs and points out the performance-enhancing elements of each.

Figure 5-1. Types of EPSSs and performance-supporting elements.

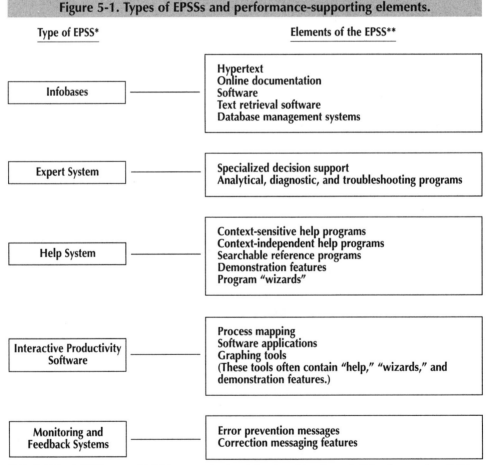

Type of EPSS*	Elements of the EPSS**
Infobases	Hypertext Online documentation Software Text retrieval software Database management systems
Expert System	Specialized decision support Analytical, diagnostic, and troubleshooting programs
Help System	Context-sensitive help programs Context-independent help programs Searchable reference programs Demonstration features Program "wizards"
Interactive Productivity Software	Process mapping Software applications Graphing tools (These tools often contain "help," "wizards," and demonstration features.)
Monitoring and Feedback Systems	Error prevention messages Correction messaging features

*Note that integrated EPSSs may contain infobases, expert systems, help systems, interactive productivity software, and monitoring and interactive feedback systems.
**Note that these elements do not constitute EPSSs in and of themselves.

As indicated in figure 5-1, expert systems simulate intelligent, problem-solving behavior such as troubleshooting. Help systems provide explanations, advice, and demonstrations for the user. Off-the-shelf productivity software often includes "help," "wizard," and demonstration features to support the user. Finally, monitoring and interactive feedback systems have error prevention and correction messaging and prompting features.

When designing and evaluating EPSSs, it is vital to remember that traditional approaches used for information technology do not apply. *Information technology focuses on functionality requirements* such as data elements, interfaces, and management reporting. In contrast, the development of an *EPSS focuses on the needs of the end user,* including work processes and ease of use. Because integrated EPSSs may include technical content, graphics, images, sounds, video clips, and animation, their development requires a team effort. The participation of development software specialists, programmers, graphic designers, technical specialists, editors, data entry specialists, project managers, and end users may be needed. Developing an EPSS may be a lengthy process, but implementing an EPSS offers many benefits to the organization:

- decreased call volume to technical support hotlines
- minimal downtime and disruption from work tasks
- immediate desktop access to the most up-to-date information available
- increased managerial control over the dissemination and maintenance of information
- decreased employee errors and mistakes
- standardization of performance across employee groups.

An Integrated Solution
The performance consultant may select EPSS from the menu of HPI interventions for solving a performance problem in situations where employees' performance depends on their ability to quickly access and interpret information, where the task is complex, or where the needed information is frequently updated or changed. In these cases, the use of a job aid or training would not effectively close the performance gap. Furthermore, when new technology is being introduced or when processes are being redesigned, an opportunity exists to develop and leverage an EPSS in support of the initiative.

Targeting Evaluation Questions
By identifying targeted evaluation questions, the performance evaluator and evaluation team can identify the relevant evaluation dimensions to include in the evaluation of EPSSs. Table 5-2 lists many examples of targeted evaluation questions, which may serve as models for evaluating EPSS in your organization. Some of the targeted evaluation questions pertain to the development of the EPSS and the user interface; others pertain to integration issues with respect to business processes and error reduction due to the EPSS.

Table 5-2. Examples of targeted evaluation questions related to EPSS.

Business Process Integration

- To what extent is the EPSS integrated with business processes?
- To what extent does the EPSS allow for the automation of manual tasks and activities?
- To what extent is the EPSS compatible with other applications, databases, and infobases used in the organization?

EPSS Development

- Was the EPSS designed and developed based on user and process requirements?
- What percentage of employees have the basic computer skills required to effectively learn the EPSS? Is formal, hands-on training planned to remediate any skill gaps before implementation of the EPSS?
- To what extent did performance consultants, information technology specialists, software specialists, programmers, graphic designers, editors, and data entry specialists collaborate in the design of the EPSS?

Error Reduction

- Does the EPSS have a built-in error detection and prevention mechanism?
- To what extent have employees' errors decreased as a result of using the EPSS?
- To what extent does the EPSS ensure standardization of performance across users?

User Interface

- To what extent are users able to navigate through the EPSS?
- How difficult is the EPSS to learn?
- Do users understand on-screen messages and prompts?
- How effective do users find the search and help features?

Evaluation Dimensions Related to EPSS

Targeting evaluation questions serves to identify the evaluation dimensions to include in an evaluation. Some evaluation dimensions to consider when evaluating an EPSS are

business process integration	organizational context
EPSS development	performance on the job
EPSS implementation	stakeholder satisfaction
EPSS maintenance	user interface
error reduction	utilization.
infobase quality	

Not all of these evaluation dimensions would be included in an evaluation; rather, the choice of evaluation dimensions to include in a given evaluation depends on stakeholder requirements and the targeted evaluation questions.

The extent of employee utilization of the EPSS may serve as the focus of the evaluation. In this case, the performance evaluator would want to determine the frequency of use of the EPSS, whether employees know how to navigate within the EPSS, whether employees possess the basic computer skills to use the EPSS, and whether any barriers to utilization exist.

Alternatively, an evaluation might focus on employee performance as a result of using the EPSS. To assess the evaluation dimension of performance on the job, the performance evaluator would need to collect key business metrics of relevance and compare these to a baseline established prior to the introduction of the EPSS. Similarly, the extent of error reduction due to employees' use of the EPSS could be examined if it were applicable.

Additionally, the process of maintaining the EPSS could be evaluated. This would involve an analysis of the procedures established to update and improve the EPSS and the frequency of these changes. An assessment might also be made of the need for future controlled releases and the development of enhanced functionality.

Is a Job Aid or EPSS the Right Intervention?

Because it is one of the least expensive HPI interventions to develop, the job aid is the most commonly used noninstructional HPI intervention. The EPSS offers an integrated approach to close performance gaps and focuses on the end user's needs, including work processes and ease of use. Because the focus is on the user's needs, performance analysis is absolutely critical before implementing these interventions.

Evaluation of these HPI interventions focuses on completeness and accuracy of the tools, ease of use, and whether they actually improve employees' performance on the job. By applying the six-step TEP process, you can gauge the quality, value, and effectiveness of job aids and EPSSs in your organizational setting.

REWARD AND INCENTIVE SYSTEMS

"The most important corporate resource over the next 20 years will be talent: smart, sophisticated business people who are technologically literate, globally astute, and operationally agile. The search for the best and the brightest will become a constant, costly battle, a fight with no final victory. Not only will companies have to devise more imaginative hiring practices; they will also have to work harder to keep their best people . . . Talent wins" (Fishman, 1998).

Strategic Questions Answered

When are reward and incentive systems designed as HPI interventions?

What are examples of both monetary and nonmonetary rewards and incentives?

What are the underlying principles of effective reward and incentive systems?

Which evaluation dimensions should be considered in evaluations of reward and incentive systems?

This chapter provides an overview of reward and incentive systems and presents targeted evaluation questions and evaluation dimensions related to this type of intervention. Many of the ideas and concepts about reward and incentive systems will be familiar to performance consultants although some may be new and or rarely thought about in the context of evaluation. These concepts provide a basis for the evaluation dimensions that are presented later in the chapter.

Reward and Incentive Systems

Reward and incentive systems compensate, encourage, and reinforce employees for their performance on the job (Wilson, 1994). In recent years employee reward and incentive systems have burgeoned both in numbers and variety. Reward and incentive systems are being structured to enhance individual, team, and organizational performance, attract new employees to the company, and retain highly skilled and talented employees. Teams are also being rewarded for accomplishing project goals and deliverables, increasing organizational productivity and performance, and implementing large-scale change initiatives. Reward and incentive systems may be available to all employees or may be developed to support an HPI project or organizational change initiative.

Reward systems that focus primarily on pay as an incentive are known as strategic pay, performance-based pay, merit pay, and competency-based pay systems. Programs that offer a range of incentives for performance are generally known as employee reward and recognition programs (E.E. Lawler, 1990; Heneman and Gresham, 1998). Because of the cost associated with providing incentives above and beyond base salary, reward and incentive programs are often designed to reward employees with critical skills and competencies that are of value to the organization (Parker and Wall, 1998). For example, a very competitive salary and bonus program may be used to attract and retain employees with critical skills, whereas a more modest salary may be offered to employees with generalized skills and competencies. Without sufficient analysis of the type of behavior that is to be rewarded, a program may inadvertently reward employees with generalized skills to stay with the company when they would likely do so without the added incentive.

A SMART Solution

To sustain or increase employee performance, effective reward and incentive programs are designed and managed with an understanding of the effect of consequences on behavior (Wilson, 1994). The four types of consequences that affect employee behavior are positive reinforcement, negative reinforcement, punishment, and extinction. With positive reinforcement, employees are encouraged to increase their performance because they receive rewards for doing so. The other consequences for behavior either diminish performance or elicit only a minimum level of performance, just enough to get by. Setting deadlines and issuing commands are forms of negative reinforcement, which results in compliance with the request. While employees do perform when negative reinforcement is used, they are not motivated to achieve more than is expected. On the other hand, punishment and extinction decrease performance altogether. Only positive reinforcement is effective in encouraging employees to go "above and beyond" and accomplish results sooner than expected because they are motivated to do so. Therefore, positive reinforcement is vital to reward and incentive programs.

In addition to serving as a source of positive reinforcement, effective reward and incentive programs must be

- *Specific.* The level of performance or desired behavior must be clearly defined and understood by employees.
- *Meaningful.* The incentive for performance should be meaningful to the recipient.
- *Achievable.* The performance must be within the employee's control or influence.
- *Reliable.* The incentive should be contingent upon the performance.
- *Timely.* The incentive should be available to the employee as soon after the performance as possible and should be provided frequently to sustain performance.

These characteristics are embedded in the acronym SMART: specific, meaningful, achievable, reliable, and timely. Research has shown that employees are motivated to perform when they believe that their performance will result in an outcome, when that outcome is attractive, and when they know that they are able to achieve the outcome (E.E. Lawler, 1998; Cummings and Worley, 1993). Ideally, there should be a strong relationship between employees' perceptions of their efforts and performance and the rewards they receive. As table 6-1 indicates, organizations use a host of rewards and incentives to encourage high levels of performance.

McKenzie and Lee (1998), among others, recommend that both monetary and nonmonetary rewards be used in a comprehensive program. The nonmonetary incentives include intrinsic rewards such as recognition for exemplary performance and opportunities for professional growth and development.

Table 6-1. Examples of monetary and nonmonetary incentives.

Monetary	Nonmonetary
Base salary	Informal acknowledgment (e.g., praise)
Commission	Formal public recognition
Individual bonus	Commendation letters
Team bonus	Advancement or promotion
Merit pay	Professional growth opportunities
Market adjustments	Mentoring
Stock options	Training and development
Profit sharing	Conference attendance
Gainsharing	More challenging assignments
Pay for specialized skills or competencies	Access to top executives
	More authority over decision making
Special awards (e.g., tickets to events, gifts)	Greater access to information
	Involvement in goal setting
Club memberships	Educational leave
	Work-related equipment (e.g., laptop computer)
	Bigger work area or office size
	Job title change
	Award dinners and celebrations
	Lunch with senior executives
	Trophies and plaques
	Company vehicle

When monetary rewards are used as part of an incentive system, they should be at least 10 to 15 percent more than the employee's base salary to effectively sustain performance over time (Boyett and Boyett, 1998). The types of monetary rewards used and how and when they are paid motivate certain behavior, and it is vital to design the program to motivate the "right" behavior. For example, to encourage employees to complete a project, team bonuses for major deliverables may be offered to motivate employees in the short term, and, as a long-term incentive, stock options may be offered at the end of the project. If the rewards are meaningful to employees, this program would serve two purposes: rewarding employees for the timely accomplishment of quarterly deliverables and rewarding employees for staying on the team through the duration of the project.

The Performance Consultant's Role in Reward and Incentive Systems
Reward and incentive systems can have a powerful effect on individual, team, and organizational performance if they are well-designed, administered, and managed. Redesigning systemwide reward and incentive systems, however, is a significant undertaking that requires the active sponsorship of executives, the support of critical business functions, such as the HR department and the legal department, and representation of employee groups. This redesign represents a fundamental change in the organization that is usually associated with organizational redesign, reengineering, or company mergers

and acquisitions. Reward and incentive programs are also designed at the business-unit level to support teamwork, collaboration, and smaller-scale change initiatives (HPI interventions, for example).

Given that reward and incentive programs are often developed in support of HPI interventions, the performance consultant is in an excellent position to assist with the design, validation, and evaluation of such programs (Kemmerer and Thiagarajan, 1992). In particular, the performance consultant can play an active role in

- establishing clear goals and objectives for the reward and incentive program
- aligning the program with the primary HPI intervention
- identifying critical skills and competencies and desired levels of performance and behavior
- establishing measures of individual, team, and organizational performance
- determining whether the incentives to be used are valued by employees
- evaluating program design, administration, and management
- determining the outcomes of the program, including any unintended effects.

Targeting Evaluation Questions
The identification of targeted evaluation questions enables the performance evaluator and evaluation team to identify the relevant evaluation dimensions to include in the evaluation of reward and incentive systems. Table 6-2 suggests some targeted evaluation questions related to reward and incentive systems. These targeted evaluation questions serve several different purposes. For example, some questions pertain to the administration and management of the reward and incentive program, whereas other questions pertain to team rewards and talent retention. Some of these targeted evaluation questions may apply to your particular evaluation effort, but you will likely need to customize the examples and create additional questions for your organization.

You will notice that the principles associated with SMART are included as evaluation questions: "Do employees feel that the rewards and incentives are worth the effort?" and "How quickly are rewards and incentives distributed and available to employees?" Perhaps a specific evaluation tool will come to mind as you answer each of the targeted evaluation questions, but tools should be selected after the targeted evaluation questions and evaluation dimensions are identified and agreed upon with stakeholders. The specific questions will depend, in part, on the original goals and objectives of the reward and incentive program and the informational needs of stakeholders.

Evaluation Dimensions Related to Reward and Incentive Systems
Targeting evaluation questions serves to identify the evaluation dimensions to include in an evaluation and vice versa. The evaluation dimensions to consider in the evaluation of reward and incentive systems are

administration and management   performance appraisal
competency   positive reinforcement

Table 6-2. Examples of targeted evaluation questions related to reward and incentive systems.

Administration and Management

- To what extent was information about the reward and incentive program available to employees?
- Were managers trained in the administration and management of the program? Were managers trained in the use of action planning as part of the performance appraisal or management system?
- To what extent were managers committed to the reward and incentive program? What factors enabled or inhibited managers' use of the reward and incentive program?

SMART

- Was the desired behavior clearly defined and understood by employees?
- Did employees feel that the rewards and incentives were worth the effort (meaningful)?
- How quickly were rewards and incentives distributed and available to employees?

Team Rewards

- Were rewards contingent upon a collaborative, effective group process?
- Were there any problems in gaining acceptance of the reward and incentive program among team members?
- To what extent did employee representatives participate in the design of the program?
- To what extent has individual and team performance improved as a result of the reward and incentive program?

Talent Retention

- Who was eligible for the reward and incentive program (which roles, critical or scarce skills, or competencies)?
- Which factors associated with job satisfaction influenced employees' intent to leave the company?
- What were the turnover rates within the organization?
- What information (reasons for leaving) was obtained from employees during employment exit interviews?

industry competition
internal equity
monetary and nonmonetary
organizational context
organizational results
performance on the job
program design
recruitment
SMART
stakeholder satisfaction
talent retention
team rewards.

Not all of these evaluation dimensions would be included in an evaluation; rather, the evaluation dimensions to be included in a given evaluation depend on stakeholder requirements and the targeted evaluation questions.

The administration and management of the reward and incentive system may be a high priority for evaluation if a new program has recently been implemented. Other evaluation dimensions to address include recruitment, talent retention, industry competition, team rewards, and stakeholder satisfaction, among others.

Reward and incentive systems can be evaluated in terms of how effectively they attract new employees to the company and retain existing employees, particularly top talent. Certainly, organizations with competitive reward and incentive systems are in a better position to attract and retain talented employees. Data from the HR function on employee turnover (voluntary turnover, termination, and so forth) can be used as an indicator of employee retention program effectiveness. If this data is not available, follow-up surveys and interviews can be conducted to gather the needed information. The direct and indirect costs of hiring and replacement can also be calculated as a cost savings or benefit associated with an effective reward and incentive system.

Competition within the industry—with respect to the monetary rewards an organization offers—is another evaluation dimension to consider when evaluating a reward and incentive system. Most organizations perform some type of compensation study every few years. Typically, a compensation analyst within the HR function collects benchmarking data from a sample of companies within the industry. With this information, the reward and incentive programs of different companies can be compared. In collaboration with the HR function, the performance consultant can assist with the evaluation of the competitiveness of rewards and incentives across the market.

Team rewards are another evaluation dimension that may be relevant to the evaluation of a reward and incentive program. The goals of rewarding group members for their contribution to team accomplishments are to foster collaboration among cross-functional teams, to increase employee problem solving, to identify process improvements within the organization, and to improve organizational performance, among other reasons. Individual, team, and organizational performance can all be used as measures of the team's success; the performance evaluator can also assess the quality of the group process and dynamics. Many instruments are available to measure the effectiveness of self-directed work teams and peers' contributions to team results; evaluation tools can be constructed as well.

Stakeholder satisfaction is another important evaluation dimension to consider with respect to reward and incentive systems. The primary stakeholder in this case is the employee. It is possible to assess employees' satisfaction with the reward and incentive program, as well as their job satisfaction in general. There are many factors associated with employees' job satisfaction; some important ones are listed in table 6-3.

For example, employees' job satisfaction correlates positively with receiving recognition for achievements and having opportunities for professional growth and development (Spector, 1997). Such factors, which serve as surrogates for job satisfaction, may be used for constructing evaluation tools.

Is a Reward and Incentive System the Right Intervention?

From a traditional compensation perspective, it almost seems silly to ask whether a reward and incentive system is the right intervention. Of course, employees expect to be compensated or remunerated for their work. To compete effectively in the global economy, however, organizations must design and implement creative reward and incentive programs to attract the best and the brightest; enhance individual, team, and organizational performance; and retain highly skilled and talented employees. Are these programs achieving their intended purpose? Table 6-4 lists a few characteristics of successful reward and incentive systems. By applying the six-step TEP, you can gauge the quality, value, and effectiveness of reward and incentive programs in your own organizational setting.

Table 6-3. Factors affecting job satisfaction.

Appreciation of effort and a job well done
Communication across the organization
Company culture
Company policies and practices
Compensation and benefits
Contact with customers
Creativity on the job
Degree of supervision
Feedback on performance
Flexible hours
Flow of information
Independence and autonomy
Interesting work
Job security
Job-related stress
Level of authority
Level of responsibility
Manager quality
Nature of the work
Need for achievement
Opportunities for personal growth
Promotion opportunities
Recognition
Relationships with co-workers
Social status
Vacations
Working close to home
Working conditions (e.g., adequacy of technology
    and equipment)
Work/life balance

Table 6-4. Lessons learned about reward and incentive systems.

1. Organizations that give the most rewards tend to attract and retain the most people.
2. Personalize rewards and incentives to recipients.
3. Reward teams for group performance to encourage collaboration.
4. Balance the provision of monetary and nonmonetary rewards.
5. Pay out rewards and incentives as frequently as possible.
6. If celebrations are planned based on major accomplishments, ensure that these activities are meaningful to employees.
7. Link managers' rewards to the performance of their work groups.
8. Display organizational results on charts and so forth as a feedback mechanism.

PROCESS IMPROVEMENT

"Process tends to be the least understood and therefore the least managed level of performance . . . The process level represents a wealth of largely untapped potential. We are learning that it is not enough to manage results. The way in which those results are achieved is also important" (Rummler and Brache, 1995).

Strategic Questions Answered

What are the different approaches to process improvement?

When is process improvement an appropriate HPI intervention?

How are business processes mapped?

What is the most important aspect of process improvement?

Which evaluation dimensions should be considered when evaluating process improvement initiatives?

This chapter provides an overview of process improvement and presents targeted evaluation questions and evaluation dimensions related to this type of intervention. Many of the ideas and concepts presented here will be familiar to the performance consultant although some may be new or rarely considered in the context of evaluation. These concepts provide a basis for identifying pertinent evaluation dimensions, which we present later in the chapter.

Process Improvement

Process improvement is a method used to improve business processes; it evolved from the quality movement of the 1980s (Harrington, Esseling, and Nimwegen, 1997). Several different approaches exist: process design, process redesign, process reengineering, benchmarking, and continuous improvement. The goal of these different approaches is to improve business processes, thereby increasing organizational performance and customer satisfaction. This chapter refers primarily to process redesign although the ideas and concepts presented are relevant to the other approaches to process improvement as well. Table 7-1 helps eliminate the confusion surrounding the different approaches to process improvement.

The major activities associated with process improvement generally involve

- securing leadership and commitment from stakeholders in support of the initiative
- documenting the existing business processes
- analyzing and designing improved processes
- implementing the improvements (changes)
- managing the new processes on an ongoing basis.

As with any HPI initiative, a clear business case must be made to justify the process redesign initiative by conducting a preliminary performance analysis. Once the business need is identified and understood, the support of leaders and stakeholders who will be affected by the initiative must be engaged. In addition to designation of a sponsor, a cross-functional team of subject matter experts and other stakeholders is established as the design

Table 7-1. Clarifying the confusion about approaches to process improvement.

Process Improvement

A method used to improve business processes through process redesign, benchmarking, reengineering, or continuous improvement; the method is also termed business process improvement.

Process Design

An approach to creating or designing new business processes that previously did not exist.

Process Redesign

An approach to redesigning existing business processes for incremental improvement.

Process Reengineering

The radical redesign of business processes for dramatic improvement.

Benchmarking

An approach to process improvement that involves studying best-in-class organizations to understand and adopt their practices and processes; it involves more than the comparative analysis of business metrics.

Continuous Improvement

An approach to organizational improvement that is conducted on an ongoing basis; this approach is similar to process redesign except that it is not limited to the improvement of processes.

team. The design team should include representatives from the various functions and groups involved in the processes to be redesigned. Ideally, these individuals should be exemplary performers who are knowledgeable about existing processes, credible within their respective departments, and able to devote significant time to the initiative. In the early stages of planning, the goals of the initiative are clearly defined and the scope of the processes is specified (that is, the process boundaries and in-scope and out-of-scope processes are defined in advance).

After establishing the design team, the existing business processes are documented in detail through in-depth interviews with employees, process walkthroughs, and review of existing documentation on work processes and procedures. Typically, an internal or external business process consultant trained in process mapping conducts the interviews and walkthroughs. Employees describe the activities, tasks, and steps that they perform in their area of the process and the problems they encounter. Because few employees understand the entire process from start to finish, interviews with multiple employees are required to gain an overall view of the process. The consultant collects metrics to indicate how the business is currently functioning in terms of effectiveness and efficiency to establish a baseline for later comparison.

After data collection, the current, or "as-is," process is mapped as a flow diagram (a process map). Many different forms of documentation are used, but the standard elements of a process map are core processes, subprocesses, inputs, outputs, customers, suppliers, decision points, and triggers; these elements are defined in table 7-2.

Various shapes and symbols represent the different elements—processes, outputs, decision points—of the process map. Arrows illustrate the sequence of activities and flow of information across the process.

To provide an overview of the entire process, a high-level process map, which includes the core processes, is drafted. From this overview, it is possible to "drill down" to greater detail on subsequent diagrams. Subprocesses, activities, tasks, and steps are revealed gradually on the more detailed diagrams. Computer icons and text on the process map indicate the tasks that are supported through technology. When the draft version of the process

Table 7-2. Standard process mapping terms.

Process	A series of sequential activities, tasks, or steps that transform inputs from suppliers into outputs for customers.
Core process	A major process that is vital to the business; core processes typically span across two or more organizational functions.
Subprocess	Part of a core process designed to accomplish a specific objective.
Input	The materials, equipment, information, and resources needed to carry out the process.
Output	The products or services that are created by the process and passed on to the customer.
Supplier	External and internal individuals who provide inputs to the process.
Customer	External and internal individuals to whom products or services are delivered.
Decision point	A point in the process where a decision must be made.
Trigger	A point in the process that signals the initiation of a simultaneous process.

map is ready, it can be created in a process-charting software application and validated with stakeholders. Some of the questions to consider when validating the process map are included in table 7-3.

The analysis and redesign of processes can begin when the existing processes are represented in a form that can be easily understood, presented, and discussed. The design team works collaboratively to identify the underlying causes of problems, eliminate barriers to the process, generate alternative solutions, and make recommendations to improve the overall process. Various strategies and tools, such as cause and effect diagrams, fishbone charts, force-field analysis, breakthrough thinking, visualization, systems thinking, and brainstorming, stimulate creative problem solving. To

Table 7-3. Validating a process map.

Although process maps vary in detail, the following questions should be useful in validating the accuracy and completeness of your "as-is" process map:

- Are the core business processes included on the process map?
- Are all subprocesses included?
- Is each activity and task in these processes included?
- Are the inputs to each activity and task identified?
- Are the outputs from each activity and task identified?
- Is the location of each activity and task noted (e.g., facility, geographical area)?
- Are all triggers in the processes identified?
- Are the major decision points in the processes identified?
- Are the decision makers noted?
- Is the length of time to complete each activity and task noted?
- Are the groups or organizations who perform the activity and task noted?
- Has the cost of performing each activity in the process been estimated (e.g., through activity-based costing)?
- Are exceptions to the process represented?
- Is the flow of information accurately illustrated?
- Is the use of technology (e.g., specific software applications) represented?
- Are the data elements that are captured, stored, or transmitted through these applications identified in supporting documentation?
- Are the technological interfaces and integration points identified in supporting documentation?
- Are the procedures represented for making changes, corrections, and updates at different points of the process?
- Are reviews, authorizations, inspections, and quality checkpoints noted?
- Are storage, waiting, or queuing delays noted?
- Are the strengths, efficiencies, and advantages of the existing process documented?

simplify business processes, the design team may recommend a host of changes including the following:

- elimination of unnecessary activities
- resequencing of activities to increase efficiency
- identification of activities that should occur simultaneously rather than sequentially
- elimination of unnecessary reviews and authorizations
- standardization of processes for consistency and quality to reduce variability in products and services
- clearer lines of decision making, authority, and accountability related to groups and roles
- use of common terminology across the business (technical procedures, acronyms, and so forth) to minimize confusion
- establishment of formal processes for making changes, corrections, or updates to information and documentation
- automation of manual processes through enabling technology
- redesign of old documents and forms
- elimination of activities that collect unused or uncommunicated data.

The team's recommendations are based upon the mission and scope of the initiative. Many factors must be considered when recommending organizational change. Once the recommendations are agreed upon, they should be represented in a future process map, which will serve as a roadmap for implementation. This map of the future, or "to-be," processes should illustrate the recommended changes and the upstream and downstream consequences of the recommended changes (Johann, 1995).

The team can develop a strategy for implementing the new processes when the future processes are conceptualized. The business owner must be committed to the implementation and play an active role in sponsoring the change. The widespread participation of stakeholders is also vital to successful implementation. At this point, project planning will be very detailed and, depending on the extent of change, organizational change management, communication, training, and HR programs will need to be designed or redesigned and implemented accordingly. As employees' roles and responsibilities change, reward and incentive programs, as discussed in chapter 6, should be considered to support the new way of doing business.

Key business metrics should be collected during implementation and compared to the baseline to measure the success of the initiative. The reporting and review of the metrics are vital to the ongoing management of the new business processes. A formal feedback system that includes designated process owners, operational reviews, and continuous improvement teams should be established to support the ongoing management of the new processes.

Harrington (1991) and Tenner and DeToro (1997) offer additional guidance on process improvement methods and techniques. These authors and Hunt (1996) provide suggestions on how to map business processes.

A Neglected Solution

Human performance improvement interventions often focus on the individual performance of employees rather than on the business processes and procedures that those employees are expected to carry out (Rummler and Brache, 1995). Although individual performance is critical to organizational effectiveness, it is not possible to maximize individuals' performance when business processes are poorly designed, inefficient, and outdated. Hence, process improvement is one of the few HPI solutions that is recommended to enhance organizational effectiveness and efficiency. Relative to the other HPI interventions presented in this book, process improvement is a significant undertaking that requires the active sponsorship of a business owner, a strategy for managing organizational change, and the alignment of related support functions within the system.

With the team approach to process improvement, the performance evaluator can provide specific competencies and expertise, which can add value to the process improvement initiative. For example, the performance evaluator can assist with the following planning and evaluation activities:

- conducting a needs assessment or performance analysis to evaluate the current performance of business processes
- establishing clear goals and objectives for the initiative
- validating the process map
- evaluating the recommendations for change based on specific criteria
- assessing the organization's readiness for change
- evaluating the implementation and results of the process improvement initiative, including any unintended effects.

Targeting Evaluation Questions

By identifying targeted evaluation questions, the performance evaluator and evaluation team can identify the relevant evaluation dimensions to include in the evaluation of process improvement initiatives. Numerous examples of targeted evaluation questions related to process improvement are presented in table 7-4. Some of these targeted evaluation questions pertain to the organization's readiness for change, some address the design team's effectiveness, and others pertain to organizational effectiveness and efficiency following implementation. Some of these targeted evaluation questions may be relevant to the evaluation of your organization's process improvement initiatives.

Evaluation Dimensions Related to Process Improvement

Targeting evaluation questions helps identify the evaluation dimensions to include in an evaluation and vice versa. The evaluation dimensions to consider in the evaluation of process improvement initiatives are

lessons learned	process management
organizational context	process mapping
organizational effectiveness	readiness for change

Table 7-4. Examples of targeted evaluation questions related to process improvement.

Readiness for Change

- Was the organization's readiness for change assessed prior to implementation?
- Was a change management plan designed and implemented to facilitate the change process?
- How were the new processes communicated throughout the organization? Was this communication delivered at the right time to the various audiences?
- Was a training program in place to train employees in the new processes and their new roles?

Team Effectiveness

- Were customers and suppliers involved in the process redesign?
- Did the design team include representatives from functional areas of the business?
- To what extent did team members fulfill their individual responsibilities?
- Did the design team use a disciplined approach to process improvement?
- Did team members learn new concepts, tools, techniques, or skills from their involvement on the project?
- Did the design team achieve the goals and performance targets they originally set?
- Was a continuous process improvement team established following implementation?

Organizational Effectiveness

- To what extent did product or service quality improve after implementation?
- Did customer satisfaction increase after implementation?
- To what extent did other organizational effectiveness measures improve from baseline after implementation?

Organizational Efficiency

- To what extent did cycle time improve after implementation?
- To what extent did product or service variability decrease after implementation?
- To what extent did other organizational efficiency measures improve from baseline after implementation?

---

organizational efficiency   stakeholder satisfaction
process design   team effectiveness.
process implementation

Not all of these evaluation dimensions would be included in an evaluation; rather, the selection of evaluation dimensions for a given evaluation depends on stakeholder requirements and the targeted evaluation questions that are posed.

Some of the evaluation dimensions are fairly obvious. For example, to evaluate stakeholder satisfaction, the design team can interview internal and external customers within the process to assess their satisfaction with the outputs they are now receiving as a result of the process redesign. Other evaluation dimensions to consider include team effectiveness, organizational effectiveness and efficiency, and process management.

Since the success of the initiative is heavily dependent on the collaboration of employees from different functions of the organization, it may be useful to formally assess the level of teamwork and collaboration that was exhibited during the design and implementation stages. The group process and dynamics might also be assessed through existing instruments. Alternatively, the design team might assess informally the effectiveness of the analysis process that it used during the redesign, the effectiveness of problem solving and brainstorming techniques, and the overall lessons learned from the experience.

The most important evaluation dimensions related to process improvement are organizational effectiveness and efficiency. Organizational effectiveness is measured through product or service quality and customer satisfaction, and organizational efficiency is measured through cycle time, service variability, or other relevant factors. As a general rule, baseline metrics should have been collected before the new processes were implemented. The effectiveness and efficiency of the organization can now be compared to the earlier baseline and to the targets that were established. You should be aware, however, of the learning curve associated with learning new processes (Harrington, Esseling, and Nimwegen, 1997). Employees' performance may diminish initially, but it will quickly improve as they become familiar with the new processes.

An evaluation may also focus on process management. In this case, the performance evaluator would begin with an examination of the performance goals that were established as a management tool, whether the goals were achieved, and whether new targets are set on an ongoing basis. The performance evaluator may also examine the continuous improvement process to determine whether information is fed back to appropriate groups for timely and effective resolution. The performance evaluator may attend operational reviews or interview the process owner to determine how resources are allocated across the business and identify any barriers to performance or "turf issues" that have arisen.

Is Process Improvement the Right Intervention?

No matter which approach—process design or redesign, process reengineering, benchmarking, or continuous improvement—is applied by your organization, the goal of process improvement is the same: to improve organizational effectiveness and efficiency (performance) and customer satisfaction. Relative to the other HPI interventions presented in this book, process improvement requires the active sponsorship of a business owner, a strategy for managing organizational change, and the alignment of related support functions within the system. Careful, up-front performance analysis must build a strong business case for such an undertaking. Compare your organization's initiatives to table 7-5, which lists some factors common to successful process improvement initiatives. By applying the six-step TEP, you can gauge the quality, value, and effectiveness of process improvement initiatives within your organizational setting.

Table 7-5. Lessons learned about process improvement.

1. Process improvement efforts should always be tied to strategic business needs; there must be a compelling business case.
2. Leaders and stakeholders need to commit to a long-term, time-consuming effort for meaningful change.
3. Minimize the number of individuals on design teams but maximize participation during implementation.
4. Design your processes first, and then select enabling technology in support of your processes.
5. The implementation of new technology alone will not result in major process improvements.
6. Organizational change management is a fundamental and critical requirement for successful implementation.
7. The consequences of process changes must be considered throughout the system. For example, the organizational structure may be reorganized, employee roles and responsibilities may change, or new competencies may need to be developed.
8. By measuring performance, you establish a basis for comparing the effectiveness and efficiency of your old processes to the new processes.

Telework and Knowledge Management

"As the 1990s draw to a close and the new millennium fast approaches, life is phenomenally interesting and demanding. Professionals who are responsible for workplace learning and performance improvement are squarely in the center of the swirl of exciting possibilities and requirements that are emerging" (Bassi, Cheney, and Lewis, 1998).

Strategic Questions Answered

What is telework?

How does telework improve performance?

When is teleworking an appropriate
HPI intervention?

What is intellectual capital?

How does intellectual capital relate to
knowledge management?

What are examples of knowledge
management interventions?

Which evaluation dimensions should be considered
when evaluating telework or knowledge management
initiatives?

Two emerging HPI solutions are presented in this chapter: telework and knowledge management. Both of these interventions are likely to become common practices in organizations in the future (Nilles, 1998; Bassi, Cheney, and Lewis, 1998). This chapter provides an overview of telework and knowledge management and presents targeted evaluation questions and evaluation dimensions related to these two interventions. Many of the ideas and concepts about telework and knowledge management may be familiar to the performance consultant, but some are new or not usually associated with evaluation. The concepts that are presented provide a basis for the evaluation dimensions that are presented later in the chapter.

Telework

With the explosion of telecommunication, computer, and Internet technology, some employees no longer have to commute to centralized work facilities or travel across the country to perform their work effectively (Nilles, 1998). Substituting technology for employee travel is central to the notion of telework. Telework is commonly known as telecommuting, although telecommuting is actually a form of telework. Unlike other forms of telework, telecommuting involves periodic work in the traditional company office, perhaps a day or two days each week. Other forms of telework include virtual teams and virtual organizations of dispersed (remote) employees (Cohen, 1997; Lipnack and Stamps, 1998). As an example of a virtual organization, Anderson Consulting has a large workforce of consultants who are located throughout the world. When consulting with their clients, their employees rely on laptop computers and Internet technology to communicate with the central office.

In general, there are two types of telework: home-based telework and telework centers. Home-based telework is the most popular and widely known form of telework. Home-based teleworkers establish an area in the home that serves as office space. All the equipment and supplies that are needed to carry out the work are available in this home office space. The other option is telework centers, which offer another way for employees to work outside the central office. Office buildings may be leased by the company to provide employees with a telework center that is close to their homes even if the main office is remote. Employees carry out their work in these centers as they would in a central office.

Not everyone in a company is eligible to participate in a telework program, however. The nature of some jobs makes them appropriate for telework whereas other jobs could not be performed effectively through telework. Jobs that are suitable for telework include software engineers and programmers, writers, consultants, analysts, and realtors. In addition, jobs that primarily involve knowledge work—retrieving and sending information, analyzing information, preparing reports, developing plans, coordinating and presenting information, or preparing communications—are well suited for telework. In addition to job type, the individual characteristics of employees must also be considered when selecting candidates for telework. The successful teleworker is self-motivated, disciplined, experienced in the role, open to change, and willing to forgo socialization with others (Nilles, 1998).

When selecting teleworkers, the organization must take into account the availability of a home-based office or telework center that has the necessary environment for effective work. For example, a telework environment should have the following: adequate work space, access to telephone and electrical outlets, secure environment for safety of documents and equipment, noise and temperature control, lighting, and separation from any ongoing domestic activities. The equipment that may be part of the telework environment include telephones (polycom); telecommunication services (multiport conference bridges); fax capability; computers with email, Internet, intranet, and local and wide area network (LAN/WAN) connections; specialized computer software; and videoconference technology (Nilles, 1998; Piskurich, 1997).

The benefits associated with telework include the following:

- improved individual and group performance
- more organizational flexibility
- faster response times
- increased teleworker morale
- more access to talent
- less employee turnover
- reduced office space requirements and energy consumption
- cleaner work environment.

Nevertheless, for telework to be successful, the organization must address several critical factors:

- careful selection of teleworkers
- establishment of a work environment conducive to telework
- training of teleworkers
- establishment of mechanisms for feedback and performance management
- management of teleworkers.

Managers of teleworkers face a challenge as they lead and manage teams of geographically dispersed employees. Managers must communicate more frequently with teleworkers and provide ongoing feedback on their performance (Nilles, 1998). Managers should have a high level of trust in their teleworkers. Organizations tend to offer telecommuting options to well-established employees whom they know well. In this case, trust has already been established and the employee has a history of effective performance.

Targeting Evaluation Questions

The identification of targeted evaluation questions enables the performance evaluator and evaluation team to identify the relevant evaluation dimensions for evaluating telework. Table 8-1 presents some examples of targeted evaluation questions related to telework. These targeted evaluation questions serve several purposes. For example, some of the questions pertain to the

Table 8-1. Examples of targeted evaluation questions related to telework.

Selecting Teleworkers

- How did employees find out about the telework program?
- Who was deemed eligible for the telework program (i.e., which roles, critical skills, or groups)?
- Were the individual characteristics of prospective teleworkers assessed before they were selected?

Telework Environment

- How effectively did teleworkers balance the responsibilities of home and work?
- Do teleworkers have well-defined areas that were treated as office space? Do teleworkers have the technology and equipment in their working environment that is necessary for effective performance?
- Does the telework environment have adequate lighting and noise control?

Telemanagement

- To what extent do managers communicate with teleworkers?
- To what extent do managers provide meaningful and challenging work assignments to teleworkers?
- How are teleworkers recognized for their achievements?
- To what extent do managers provide specific, measurable, and attainable standards of performance?
- Do managers focus on results (deliverables) rather than processes?

Performance on the Job

- Compared to traditional employees, how did the performance of teleworkers compare?
- To what extent are teleworkers able to balance the responsibilities of home and work?
- What factors directly influenced the success of the telework program?

selection of teleworkers, some address the telework environment, and other questions relate to the management and performance of teleworkers.

Evaluation Dimensions Related to Telework

The process of targeting evaluation questions helps identify evaluation dimensions to include in an evaluation and vice versa. The evaluation dimensions to consider in the evaluation of telework are

organizational context	talent retention
organizational results	technology
performance on the job	telemanagement
recruitment	telework environment
selecting teleworkers	training teleworkers.
stakeholder satisfaction	

Not all of these evaluation dimensions would be included in an evaluation; rather, the selection of evaluation dimensions for an evaluation depends on stakeholder requirements and the targeted evaluation questions. Among the most important evaluation dimensions are the selection and training of teleworkers (discussed earlier), stakeholder satisfaction, and telemanagement.

Any evaluation can gauge stakeholder satisfaction. In the case of telework, teleworkers' satisfaction with the new working arrangements can be assessed in a variety of ways. For example, it may be important to assess teleworkers' satisfaction with the management they receive (for example, the frequency of communication and feedback, the nature of the work, and the assigned workload). These questions are important since research has shown that managers tend to impose unreasonable deadlines on teleworkers and that teleworkers end up working excessive hours to overcome any negative perception of their productivity (Huws et al., 1996).

Telemanagement is another evaluation dimension to consider. Managing a virtual team of teleworkers can be challenging without face-to-face contact. Three factors associated with effective telemanagement are communication, trust, and an emphasis on results. Experienced employees tend to be the best candidates for telework because they already have a track record and have established trust and credibility within their organization. In addition to establishing trust and communicating frequently, it is recommended that telemanagers focus on the end product rather than on the process (the way that the teleworker carries out the work). This focus on deliverables minimizes conflict and causes less hassle for managers; it also gives teleworkers more flexibility in how they do their jobs.

Knowledge Management

Recent and growing interest has promoted the notion of intellectual capital and knowledge management. Intellectual capital refers to the knowledge, talents, and capabilities that exist and are valued within an organization. These talents and capabilities are important assets that can give an organization a competitive advantage. Knowledge management is the process by which an organization captures, manages, and leverages intellectual capital. Table 8-2 introduces some terminology that pertains to these two concepts.

Since many of these concepts are relatively new and abstract, organizations are just beginning to find ways to measure or quantify them. Table 8-3 provides some example metrics for human, structural, and customer capital.

As an example of the measurement of human capital, the average seniority of employees within a company can be calculated as an indictor of the relative experience employees possess. Similarly, the number of employees

Table 8-2. Knowledge management terminology.

Intellectual Capital	Knowledge that is of value to the organization, including human capital, structural capital, and customer capital (Stewart, 1997; Bassi, 1997)
Human Capital	A category of intellectual capital that is associated with employees' knowledge, skill, competency, and innovation; it also includes the organization's culture, values, and philosophy
Structural Capital	A category of intellectual capital that includes hardware, software, databases, organizational structure, business processes, patents, trademarks, and copyrights that are owned by the organization (Edvinsson and Malone, 1997)
Customer Capital	A category of intellectual capital that includes customer information such as purchasing patterns, financial stability, customer satisfaction, loyalty to products, and information about the market (Bassi, 1997)
Tacit Knowledge	Informal knowledge based on intuition, values, beliefs, and experience, and that is difficult to articulate and communicate to others (Nonaka and Takeuchi, 1996)
Explicit Knowledge	More formal knowledge that is easily shared and articulated; this type of knowledge can be quantified more readily than tacit knowledge
Knowledge Repositories	Knowledge and information that is stored (e.g., in databases or on intranets) for employees to retrieve
Knowledge Transfer	The formal process of sharing and using knowledge across the organization through human interaction; knowledge transfer may be facilitated by the use of technology
Organizational Learning	The intentional use of learning processes at the individual, group, and system level to continuously transform the organization in a direction that is increasingly satisfying to stakeholders (Dixon, 1994); it involves learning from past successes and failures, critical thinking, risk-taking and innovation, and the exchange of ideas throughout the organization

Table 8-3. Examples of intellectual capital metrics.

Human Capital	Structural Capital	Customer Capital
Employees (#)	Time to market (#)	Customer satisfaction indices (%)
Seniority of employees (#)	Business processes (#)	Customer product loyalty indices (%)
Average age of employees (#)	Trademarks, patents, and copyrights (#)	Competitor information (#, %)
Employee turnover (%)	Business licenses (#)	Market coverage (%)
Employee satisfaction indices (%)	Information systems and databases (#)	Benchmarking data (#, %)
Diversity indices (%)	Computers per employee (#)	Customer contracts (#)
Rookie ratio (employees with less than two years' experience) (%)	Employee profiles and skill inventory databases (%)	Market trends (%)
Employee computer literacy indices (%)		
Human resource development expense per employee ($)		
Employees with college and advanced degrees (#)		

with college degrees is an indicator of knowledge that was formally acquired through education. Employee satisfaction can also be measured as an indicator of the stability of this human capital (i.e., the extent to which employees are dissatisfied and likely to leave, taking their knowledge and experience with them).

Examples of measures of structural capital include the number of computers, information systems, and databases available to employees. Measures of customer capital include indices of customer satisfaction, the number of customer contracts awarded annually, and the company's share in the market. These indicators, or metrics, are only meaningful in relation to other metrics and are used primarily for planning purposes (Hackett, 1997).

The balanced scorecard is one framework that can be used to present key business metrics, such as measures of intellectual capital, to stakeholders (Kaplan and Norton, 1996). Three of the four broad measures in the balanced scorecard are learning and growth, internal business, and customers. These measures correlate with the measures of intellectual capital. The fourth broad measure in the balanced scorecard represents financial measures. Although financial measures are not directly relevant to intellectual capital, they are of interest to stakeholders in relation to the measures of intellectual capital. Frameworks, such as the balanced scorecard, are useful to attain a basic understanding of the intellectual capital that is valued in the organization, but other milestones of success become important once the knowledge management initiative is under way (Davenport and Prusak, 1998).

Once the intellectual capital of the organization is assessed, strategies can be developed to capture, manage, and leverage this knowledge to enable the organization to become more competitive. One way to capture knowledge is to through knowledge repositories. Knowledge repositories can be designed to house company libraries, competitor information, market updates, reports, and so forth. By using a knowledge repository, such as a database, and a sourcing capability, such as a Web interface, employees can easily store and retrieve information. Although it is relatively easy to store information through technology, storing information is not knowledge management per se. Technology can facilitate other knowledge management strategies, including

- an employee skills tracking database based on employees' online self-assessments
- external Internet access to help employees access industry knowledge, competitor information, and so forth
- a set of commonly used software for word processing, presentations, and email so that documents and information can be easily exchanged
- an intranet search engine for easy document retrieval and downloading.

Knowledge transfer is critical to the creation of new knowledge and the sharing and use of existing knowledge. Although spontaneous knowledge transfer between employees is important, it tends to happen only locally in fragmented fashion. Knowledge transfer does not have to be a formalized process, but specific strategies should be developed to encourage spontaneous sharing and receptivity to information exchange (Fisher and Fisher, 1998). Davenport and Prusak (1998) provide strategies for designing knowledge management initiatives. Some examples of these strategies are

- institutionalizing a lessons-learned meeting as a project-completion deliverable
- sponsoring open forums, colloquiums, and knowledge fairs
- establishing an expert exchange program between business groups or organizations to promote cross-functional collaboration and knowledge transfer.

Targeting Evaluation Questions
The identification of targeted evaluation questions enables the performance evaluator and evaluation team to identify the relevant evaluation dimensions to include in the evaluation of knowledge management. Table 8-4 presents many examples of targeted evaluation questions related to knowledge management. Some of these questions may pertain to your evaluation of knowledge management initiatives. These targeted evaluation questions address different aspects of knowledge management. For example, some of these questions pertain to the culture within the organization, some are related to measuring and tracking intellectual capital, and others are related to knowledge transfer and the use of enabling technology.

Evaluation Dimensions Related to Knowledge Management

Targeting evaluation questions serves to identify the evaluation dimensions to include in an evaluation and vice versa. The evaluation dimensions to consider in the evaluation of knowledge management initiatives are

collaboration and teamwork
intellectual capital
knowledge transfer
knowledge repositories
organizational context
organizational culture

enabling technology
organizational learning
organizational results
stakeholder satisfaction
work environment.

Table 8-4. Examples of targeted evaluation questions related to knowledge management.

Organizational Culture

- To what extent does the organizational culture encourage employees to seek out, create, and share knowledge?
- To what extent does the organizational culture encourage risk taking and innovation?
- Is the employee reward and incentive system aligned with the knowledge management initiative? To what extent are employees rewarded for sharing knowledge?

Intellectual Capital

- Do executives and senior managers recognize the benefit of tracking intellectual capital measures as well as financial measures?
- Is a balanced set of measures tracked? Are these measures perceived to be meaningful within the organization? What does the data suggest or imply?
- Are the measures used for organizational change and performance improvement?

Knowledge Transfer

- To what extent are employees encouraged to share knowledge across business groups and functions?
- Are cross-functional teams encouraged to capture and disseminate lessons learned from projects and initiatives?
- What types of meetings (e.g., open forums, knowledge fairs) are used to promote knowledge transfer?
- Have any self-organizing (i.e., informal) networks of knowledge transfer emerged?
- How does the organization encourage relationships with external knowledge providers (conferences, research centers, universities)?

Enabling Technology

- Does the organization have enabling technology to support knowledge transfer?
- To what extent is this technology used? How effective is this technology (e.g., accessibility, response time, capacity, and so forth)?
- Do knowledge workers (employees) have access to the Internet?

Not all of these evaluation dimensions would be included in an evaluation; rather, the selection of evaluation dimensions for an evaluation depends on stakeholder requirements and the targeted evaluation questions. The performance evaluator can include evaluation dimensions to assess employees' awareness of and access to knowledge repositories. The usefulness of the information in knowledge repositories might also be evaluated along with the procedures for selecting this information. Interviews with managers responsible for the administration and maintenance of these repositories would likely reveal additional valuable information about employee usage of knowledge repositories.

A second evaluation dimension to consider when evaluating a knowledge management initiative is knowledge transfer—the sharing and exchange of knowledge among employees, teams, and business groups. The performance evaluator can conduct interviews or surveys to assess both formal and informal mechanisms of knowledge transfer within the organization and the perceived usefulness of these mechanisms.

Is Telework or Knowledge Management the Right Answer?

Telework and knowledge management are emerging HPI solutions. As such, organizations are just beginning to offer telework alternatives, measure intellectual capital, and design knowledge management initiatives. Evaluation of these innovative HPI solutions is an evolving science, but already some characteristics common to successful knowledge management programs are known (table 8-5). The examples of targeted evaluation questions and evaluation dimensions offered in this chapter can guide performance evaluators who are embarking on evaluation of telework and knowledge management initiatives. Following the six-step TEP can help evaluators build a business case based on quality, value, and effectiveness.

Table 8-5. Lessons learned about knowledge management.

1. Start with knowledge that is of value to the organization.
2. Foster an awareness of the value of knowledge and be willing to invest in the process of creating it.
3. Build trust through face-to-face meetings; knowledge sharing requires trust.
4. Create a common ground between business groups and organizations through education, discussion, teaming, knowledge fairs, and so forth.
5. Provide time for learning.
6. Reward knowledge sharing.
7. Accept creative errors and collaboration.
8. Develop strategies on multiple fronts (e.g., technology, organizational culture, formal networks).
9. Solicit help from stakeholders throughout the organization.

Davenport and Prusak, 1998

PART 3

MECHANICS OF THE TEP

DESIGNING THE TOOLS, TECHNOLOGY, AND TECHNIQUES

"Evaluation continues to become ever more methodologically diverse. It is by now well established that the full array of social science methods belongs in the evaluator's tool kit . . ." (Chelimsky and Shadish, 1997).

Strategic Questions Answered

Which evaluation tools are available to the performance evaluator?

How is each tool developed and customized?

When should technology be used with these tools?

Which evaluation techniques are often overlooked by inexperienced performance evaluators?

Why are tool reliability and validity so important?

Earlier in the book, we introduced the basics of HPI and the TEP. We also described several common HPI interventions and how performance evaluators can apply the TEP with these interventions. We provided some specific examples of targeted evaluation questions and evaluation dimensions for each intervention. This part of the book, explains the last three steps of the TEP in greater detail. These steps are

- designing the tools, technology, and techniques (step 4)
- gathering and analyzing data (step 5)
- reporting results (step 6).

Although much has been written about these steps—the "mechanics" of evaluation—we have placed these well-known practices into the context of the TEP as suggested in this book, placing special emphasis on tying these steps to the targeted evaluation questions and evaluation dimensions.

Evaluation Tools

The selection and design of the tools and technology to use in an evaluation is presented in this chapter as step 4 of the TEP. The tools that you select and design will, of course, depend on the targeted evaluation questions and evaluation dimensions for the evaluation. These tools include surveys, interviews, observations, focus groups, knowledge and performance assessments, and key business metrics. We explain the steps involved in designing and customizing tools along with the advantages and disadvantages of each. Because myriad technological formatting options are now available, we present several options for designing these evaluation tools. In addition, we explain three techniques that are useful for evaluation. These concern the evaluation design, sampling strategy, and tool quality.

Surveys

One of the tools used in the evaluation of HPI interventions is the survey. Surveys allow you to collect information related to an intervention from a large number of people relatively easily. Surveys can be designed in different technological formats, but the general steps for constructing a survey remain the same:

1. Generate survey items (questions or statements), and group them into categories.
2. Select appropriate response alternatives.
3. Include directions on how to complete the survey.
4. Design the layout and technology, if applicable.
5. Review with stakeholders, conduct a pilot test, and revise the survey.

The first step is to generate the items (questions) to be posed on the survey. These should correlate with the targeted evaluation questions and evaluation dimensions for the evaluation. Brainstorming is a good way to generate such items. After a pool of items is created, the items should be categorized under headings, and any redundant or unnecessary items eliminated. Table 9-1 presents a checklist of questions to consider in constructing and revising surveys.

Once the items have been constructed, the response alternatives to be used with each item are selected. Not all items on the survey will necessarily use the same response alternative. The different response alternatives typically used on surveys include the following: rating scales, multiple choice, binary (yes/no or true/false questions), ranking, checklist, and open-ended (short answer). The two that are most frequently used are closed-ended items with rating scales and open-ended items. Individuals must choose from a list of specified response alternatives to respond to closed-ended items. Table 9-2 shows examples of different rating scales.

The labels in table 9-2 add meaning to the numbers on the scale. Note that the response alternatives are equivalent on each side of the scales. For example, the response "strongly disagree" is equivalent to "strongly agree." Three- and five-point rating scales are illustrated in table 9-2, but longer scales can be used. With a longer scale (for example, a nine-point scale), more discrimination among responses is possible. Furthermore, using an even-numbered scale forces respondents to select one side of the scale over the other, rather than a middle point. Open-ended items allow individuals to write a response to the item in their own words. The length of the line or size of the blank space after the item is a cue to suggest an appropriate length for the respondent's comments. Open-ended items are appropriate to use when the performance evaluator is unsure of all of the possible responses that individuals may give.

Open-ended items on surveys can lead to some complications. For example, people may respond with information that is only indirectly related to the question. Written responses are also difficult to decipher and may be incomplete or ambiguous. Furthermore, respondents often leave open-ended items blank because they do not want to take the time to write out a response.

No matter which type of response alternative is used, it is important to specify how the respondent should answer each item. For example, if an item pertains to professional position, all possible positions should be represented in the response alternatives. Respondents should also be alerted to the number of responses that are appropriate for each item ("circle one" or

Table 9-1. Checklist for constructing a survey instrument.

	YES	NO
Items		
Are the items related to the targeted evaluation questions and evaluation dimensions being evaluated?	(✓)	( )
Are items written in simple sentences of 20 words or fewer?	( )	( )
Are the items limited to those that are necessary?	( )	( )
Does each item represent a single idea?	( )	( )
Have leading words and phrases been eliminated?	( )	( )
Has the use of technical jargon been avoided?	( )	( )
Are absolute terms, such as "all" or "none," avoided?	( )	( )
Is bias avoided in reference to gender?	( )	( )
Is the level of reading difficulty appropriate for the audience?	( )	( )
Response Alternatives		
Are all possible response alternatives listed?	( )	( )
Are Likert-type scale response alternatives symmetrical with as many positive choices as negative?	( )	( )
Should "not applicable" be added as a response alternative?	( )	( )
Has "neutral" been avoided as a response alternative?	( )	( )
Is the number of responses to be given clearly identified for each item (e.g., "check all that apply")?	( )	( )
Grouping and Sequencing		
Are similar items grouped together in categories?	( )	( )
Are items with the same type of response alternative grouped together?	( )	( )
Do the items flow in a logical sequence from general to specific within categories?	( )	( )
Are major areas covered thoroughly and minor areas covered quickly?	( )	( )
Are demographic items located at the end of the survey?	( )	( )
Directions to Respondents		
Have the purpose, sponsor, and limits of confidentiality been explained?	( )	( )
Are the directions for completing the survey clear and concise?	( )	( )
Are definitions included for ambiguous items and response alternatives?	( )	( )
Are the instructions for returning the survey and the due date specified, if the survey is not group-administered?	( )	( )
Layout		
Is the font easy to read and attractive in terms of size and spacing?	( )	( )
Are underlining, italics, and boldface fonts used to make distinctions between items?	( )	( )
Would the use of borders simplify the layout?	( )	( )

Table 9-2. Labels for rating scales.

5-point rating scales				
(1) -------- (2) ------- (3) ------- (4) ------- (5)				
Strongly Disagree	Disagree	Neither Disagree nor Agree	Agree	Strongly Agree
Very Dissatisfied	Dissatisfied	Neither Dissatisfied nor Satisfied	Satisfied	Very Satisfied
Not at all	To a little extent	To some extent	To a great extent	To a very great extent
Not important	Somewhat important	Important	Very important	Extremely important
Very low	Low	Moderate	High	Very high
Substantially worse	Somewhat worse	About the same	Somewhat better	Substantially better
3-point rating scales				
(1) ------------ (2) ------------ (3)				
Decrease		Remain the same		Increase
Too short		Just right		Too long

"check all that apply"). Finally, response alternatives should match the respective item; that is, the response alternatives should be appropriate to the survey item.

Directions on how to complete the survey and the time that it will take should be clearly visible on the front of the survey. Make clear the purpose of the survey and identify the business owner or sponsor so that respondents understand the goal of the survey tool. Define important terms or concepts to ensure that respondents have a shared understanding of the meaning of items. If the survey is not administered in a group setting, directions for the return of the survey and the date that it is due should be clearly visible on the survey. The demographic items should be the last items on the survey because respondents are more likely to complete a survey when personal questions are asked last (Fowler, 1993).

The layout of the survey is the final consideration. The font should be easy to read and attractive in size and shape. Underlining, italics, or boldface type can be used to make distinctions between items and enhance the overall look of the survey. Layout decisions should be based, at least in part, on the technology used; for example, formatting may be limited if optical scanning technology is used. When the survey is in final form, stakeholders should review it to determine if it meets their informational needs. It is important to pilot test all surveys to identify errors and make improvements before mass production.

The performance evaluator must weigh additional considerations when designing an online survey:

1. Add a Website visitor counter to compare the number of visits to the site with the number who actually completed the survey.
2. Include an "other" response alternative as often as possible to allow respondents to answer with responses that are not included as options.
3. Allow respondents to change their answer by hitting a "clear" button to change a response before submitting the survey; the "clear" button should just clear the item or section and not the entire survey.
4. Indicate the number of words expected for answers to open-ended questions (for example, 25 words or fewer) to limit response length.
5. If demographic information is critical, include an error message if this information is not completed with the item number that is incomplete.
6. Include a message to the respondent to confirm the submission of the survey.
7. Thank the respondents for their time and reiterate how the information will be used at the end of the survey.
8. If survey questions are changed frequently, include a message with the date the survey was last updated.

The survey as an evaluation tool has several advantages and disadvantages. The obvious advantage is the relative ease in collecting a large amount of information in a relatively short period of time. Since the survey is designed in-house, targeted evaluation questions can be identified and included on the survey. An additional advantage is the availability of technology to make the survey process quicker. The major disadvantage associated with the use of surveys is the low return rate and incomplete data. Nevertheless, the survey is the most widely used tool for evaluation. Examples of the multiple uses of surveys in evaluation are

- a survey of trainees used to measure the extent to which skills learned in training transferred to the work environment by including questions on the relevance of training to the job, the opportunity to perform, barriers to performance, and confidence in performance
- a rating form for performers to measure the extent to which a job aid facilitated performance on the job by including questions pertaining to the accessibility, frequency of use, and ease of use of the job aid
- a survey of managers' current practices related to an employee reward and incentive program through questions about administration of the program and consistency of use
- a self-reported skills assessment for employees to document their areas of expertise and competence.

Interviews

Conducting interviews is another way to collect information for evaluating HPI interventions. Interviews may be conducted in person or over the telephone. When used as a source of evaluative information, interviews should be performed in a consistent manner so that results can be quickly collated and compared. The steps in preparing for interviews are

1. Choose method for interview: in-person or telephone.
2. Generate the interview questions and arrange in a logical sequence, thereby creating an interview script.
3. Select open-ended or closed-ended format and construct the recording form.
4. Prepare standard interview instructions; formulate a list of questions that respondents may ask and appropriate responses.
5. Review interview script with stakeholders, conduct pilot test, and revise as necessary.
6. Train the interviewers.

The first step is to decide whether to conduct the interview in person or over the telephone. Interviewing over the telephone is less costly since travel to participants' work sites is not required. The telephone interview is also quicker and more convenient for respondents.

After a decision is made about whether to conduct interviews in person or over the telephone, the questions to be asked are generated. The questions should be written in a natural conversational tone and should be simple enough for the interviewer to read to the respondent without the respondent forgetting any part. Since the respondent cannot see the interview script, the success or failure of the interview depends on the interviewer's ability to present the items and response alternatives in a clear, complete manner. All respondents should be asked the same questions in the same way so that responses are comparable.

After the interview script is generated, a concomitant recording form is created. The recording form is used to code or write in respondents' answers. On open-ended questions, respondents' answers should be recorded completely. The interviewer may need to ask clarifying questions during the interview if vague or incomplete answers are given. These probes should be listed on the interviewing script. Instructions to the interviewer about how to establish rapport and explain the purpose of the interview and how the data will be used should also be included. It is also wise to create a list of questions that respondents are likely to ask about the interviewing process along with the answers so that interviewers know how to respond.

It is vital that interviewers receive training about interviewing techniques. Otherwise, interviewers may inadvertently bias the data gathering. For example, one interviewer may ask questions more enthusiastically than another and obtain different results. Training should minimize such influences. Additionally, a simple statistical test can determine if the bias is associated with a particular interviewer. This statistic (inter-rater reliability) will be discussed in a subsequent section of this chapter.

The interview tool offers many advantages to the performance evaluator. Because the interviewer can ask questions of the respondent, it is possible to clarify answers and probe for more detail. Interviewing, however, is relatively time consuming; just scheduling an interview may require several contacts. Providing advance notice of the interview, limiting its length, and scheduling the interview at a time that is convenient to the respondent increases the likelihood that individuals will participate in an interview.

Examples of the use of the interviewing tool for evaluation include the following:

- Employees involved in an on-the-job computer training program are interviewed in person after a performance assessment during which they demonstrated their newly acquired skills.
- Quick telephone interviews are conducted with a representative sample of employees to determine whether they had received and used a new job aid consisting of a procedural checklist.
- An external company is contracted to interview customers to determine their level of satisfaction with a new service program.

Focus Groups

The focus groups is another tool for evaluating HPI interventions by exploring an issue in depth. The questions posed during focus groups require reflective thought and interaction and, for this reason, only a few questions should be addressed during a standard session. The strategy for the session is designed in advance to ensure that the results of the focus group are meaningful. As an evaluation tool, focus groups can examine stakeholders' observations and experiences related to an HPI intervention.

The steps in designing a focus group are

1. Define the purpose of the session.
2. Identify participants and the number of sessions required.
3. Generate a list of sufficiently complex, open-ended questions, and arrange them in a logical sequence.
4. Design the strategy for stimulating discussion.
5. Prepare a session agenda and any accompanying handouts.
6. Review the strategy with stakeholders, conduct a pilot test, and modify as needed.

Defining the purpose of the focus group session is the first step of the process. The purpose depends on the targeted evaluation questions and evaluation dimensions of interest. When the purpose of the session is established, the specific questions for the session and the strategy for eliciting discussion are designed. Both the design of the session and the skills of the moderator are critical to the success of the focus group. Without sufficient preparation and facilitation skill, the data from the focus group may not be meaningful or useful.

The moderator should create a permissive, nonthreatening atmosphere in which participants feel free to discuss their observations and experiences related to the intervention. At the start of the session, the moderator should identify the sponsor and purpose of the session and describe how the information will be used. The moderator also outlines the agenda and provides background information about the intervention for the group. To facilitate the group discussion, the moderator asks for clarification and elaboration as necessary.

Those who were involved in or affected by the intervention (employees, managers, and customers) are usually selected to participate in focus groups. It may be necessary to conduct several different groups to keep the groups small and appropriately grouped. Ideally, the focus group should be limited to six to 12 individuals so that questions and issues can be thoroughly explored. Individuals should be grouped together based on similarities. For example, managers should participate in one session and employees in another.

The advantage of the focus group as an evaluation tool is the opportunity to explore an issue in greater depth than is possible through other evaluation tools. As the group discusses the intervention, the moderator can seek clarification and focus the group to gather important information. Through this method, issues that were not originally anticipated may be uncovered. A potential disadvantage associated with the focus group tool is the potential for the moderator to inadvertently bias the group discussion. Generally, participants benefit from listening to one another and interacting, but sometimes participants are unduly influenced by others, or, in some cases, one or more participants dominate the discussion. As a caution, the information that is collected through the use of focus groups may be very descriptive. This information can be very useful, but it may reveal negative information—not anticipated by stakeholders—about the intervention.

Examples of different types of focus groups include the following:

- A focus group may be designed to identify the source of problems that have arisen during the implementation of an intervention and to explore potential solutions; one session may include managers and a second session may include front-line employees.
- Another focus group may be designed to elicit observations of the effects of the intervention, both direct and indirect; managers may be selected as participants for this session.
- A third focus group may be designed to identify the lessons learned from an intervention and to make recommendations for future interventions; the participants in this session may include program stakeholders, designers, and performance consultants.

Observation

Observation is another useful tool for evaluating HPI interventions. Observation involves first-hand examination of an object—an activity, process, behavior, performance, work sample, or product. Certain important features of the object are described or rated on a checklist or rating form. Observation is appropriate when the object can be readily and directly observed; observation is not appropriate for examining subtle changes or complex activities. A structured approach to observation involves the following steps:

1. Identify the object (activity, process, behavior, performance, work sample, or product) to be observed.
2. List the discrete events or elements to be observed and organize in a progressive or logical order.
3. Construct the observation form, including rating scales and checklists.
4. Include instructions on how to complete the observation.
5. Conduct a pilot test and revise the observational form.
6. Train the observers.

Checklists and rating scales can be used to aid the observation. The performance evaluator can use checklists to document required elements (for example, whether a product meets or does not meet a predetermined quality or performance standard). In contrast, rating scales enable the observer to discriminate among levels of quality. For example, the observer may note that "the product meets 50 (or 75 or 100) percent of the criteria." Any given observation form may have a number of both checklist and rating scale items. Explicit instructions on how to perform the observation and complete the rating form should be covered during the observers' training. If more than one individual rates an object, inter-rater reliability should be calculated using the statistical test described later in this chapter.

Individuals who will be observed should be informed in advance of the purpose and timing of the observation. Of course, the observer should not give directions, answers, or nonverbal cues while observing performance. Since observation can be threatening to employees, observers should attempt to minimize their influence.

Some examples of how observation can be used for evaluation are

*   documenting the original performance gap (e.g., performance of average and exemplar performers) as part of the performance analysis stage of the HPI process
*   verifying or double-checking events reported on other evaluation tools
*   comparing work samples or outputs to quality standards and then rating the sample or output accordingly.

Knowledge and Performance Assessments

Performance evaluators can use two types of assessments or tests to evaluate the effectiveness of HPI interventions. Knowledge assessments are designed to measure learning, and performance assessments are designed to measure skill. Knowledge and performance assessments are typically used in the evaluation of instructional rather than noninstructional interventions.

The steps involved in constructing either type of assessment are

1. Review the objectives of the intervention.
2. Generate list of items to be learned or skills to be mastered.
3. Break skills down into task elements.
4. Arrange items or tasks in a logical sequence.
5. Determine correct answers or describe standards or criteria of performance.
6. Include instructions on how to complete the assessment.
7. Pilot test the assessment to check reliability and validity.
8. Establish cutoff scores, standards, or criteria of performance.

The items on the knowledge assessment should represent the most important learning objectives of the intervention. Similarly, the skills included on the performance assessment should represent the most critical skills to be mastered as a result of the intervention. Additional considerations in the construction of knowledge and performance assessments are listed in table 9-3.

On performance assessments, the standard of performance for each skill should be clearly identified next to each skill to be performed. Checklists and rating scales, similar to those used on observational forms, can be used with items (skills) on the performance assessment to check off or rate performance.

Knowledge and performance assessments should always be fair, objective, reliable, and valid (Westgard, 1999). Therefore, it is essential to conduct pilot tests of assessments to identify items that should be revised or omitted altogether. The level of difficulty of each item should also be determined through item analysis to verify that items appear in order of increasing difficulty. Instructions for conducting item analysis are presented in chapter 10.

Key Business Metrics

As an alternative to designing tools specifically for an evaluation, it may be appropriate to track key business metrics that are relevant to the HPI intervention. Various functions throughout the organization are probably collecting and reporting such business metrics. Examples of key business metrics are accuracy; benchmarking; customer satisfaction; efficiency; finances and costs; performance and effectiveness; trends or historical data; productivity and quantities; quality; and time.

Within each of the key business metrics is a number of specific measures that depend largely on the type of business. For example, quality measures may include percentage of conformance to specifications, durability, and ease of use; accuracy measures may include percentage of defective material, error rates, and amount of time spent reprocessing or reworking orders; and customer satisfaction measures may include accessibility, responsiveness, and reliability. The way in which a measure is operationalized (that is, defined) depends on the business and intervention. No matter which key business metrics are used, they should be accurate, reliable, and timely to be deemed credible by business sponsors and owners.

Table 9-3. Checklist for constructing knowledge and performance assessment tools.

	YES	NO
Knowledge Assessments		
Are items based on the learning objectives of the intervention?	(✓)	( )
Are the items limited to the most important ones?	( )	( )
Are items written in simple and concise language?	( )	( )
Are items arranged from easy to difficult?	( )	( )
Is the meaning of items clear without reading the response alternatives?	( )	( )
Have ambiguous terms been eliminated from items and response alternatives?	( )	( )
Have double negatives been eliminated from items and response alternatives?	( )	( )
Are the response alternatives similar in length?	( )	( )
Are the incorrect response alternatives plausible?	( )	( )
Are "all of the above" and "none of the above" responses avoided?	( )	( )
Are items with the same type of response alternatives grouped together?	( )	( )
Is the order of answers random across items?	( )	( )
Does the assessment discriminate among participants?	( )	( )
Have items that nearly everyone misses been omitted?	( )	( )
Are the directions for completing the assessment conspicuous and explicit?	( )	( )
Performance Assessments		
Are the skills to be performed based on the objectives of the intervention?	( )	( )
Are the skills to be performed limited to those which are most critical?	( )	( )
Is each skill broken down to the task level?	( )	( )
Is the meaning of tasks clear?	( )	( )
Are the tasks arranged in a logical sequence?	( )	( )
Is the standard of performance clearly specified?	( )	( )
Is the standard of performance realistic?	( )	( )
Are the conditions clearly specified (e.g, use of a manual, online documentation, or a job aid)?	( )	( )
Are important terms on the assessment defined?	( )	( )
Are the instructions to the rater conspicuous and explicit?	( )	( )

The balanced scorecard approach (Kaplan and Norton, 1996) focuses on organizational performance in four broad areas: financial; internal business; customer; and learning and growth. In using the framework, organizations report on key business metrics within each of these four areas. Performance targets, which are linked to organizational strategies and objectives, are then set. The performance measures collected and reported through the balanced scorecard approach are broad measures. As such, they may be too high-level to detect any improvements in performance that result from small-scale interventions. Hence, the usefulness and interpretability of these global measures may be limited in the evaluation of certain interventions.

Examples of the use of key business metrics in the evaluation of HPI interventions include the following:

- measurement of cycle time (an efficiency metric) following business process improvements in a manufacturing business unit
- measurement of daily group quotas achieved (a productivity metric) as a result of the implementation of a reward program for telemarketers
- reduction in the number of payroll errors (an accuracy metric) as a result of a cross-training intervention in a business office
- increased conformance to specifications (a quality metric) after the introduction of an online software tool (EPSS) in a product-ordering department.

Choosing an Evaluation Tool

The performance evaluator must choose from a number of evaluation tools when implementing the TEP. Table 9-4 summarizes the major advantages and disadvantages of each tool. Ultimately, the choice of which tool or tools to use should be based on the targeted evaluation questions and evaluation dimensions for the evaluation. Furthermore, the performance evaluator must consider stakeholders' perceptions of the credibility of the selected tool.

Technology

Recent advances in technology have led to many new ways of designing and administering evaluation tools. For example, as alternatives to the traditional paper-and-pencil surveys or assessments, evaluation tools can be designed through Internet software, optical scanning technology, and other advancements. New techniques in telephone polling allow completely automated telephone interviewing. Many suppliers display these technologies every year at conference expositions. The ease of use, resources required, costs, and limits to confidentiality associated with six technologies are presented in table 9-5.

Some examples of how technology is used in evaluation are

- scannable survey of trainees used to measure the extent to which skills learned in training transferred to the job
- online rating forms for performers to rate the extent to which a job aid improved performance on the job

Table 9-4. Common evaluation tools.

Tool	Purpose	Requirements	Advantages	Disadvantages
Surveys	To collect information from many respondents through paper-based or technological means	Construction of survey Follow-up contact with individuals who have not returned the survey (if not group-administered)	Wide array of alternative formats: paper, scannable forms, computer-based-training embedded surveys, email, fax, automated telephone, and intra/Internet technology Response alternatives vary: Likert-type scales, open-ended, etc. Easy and cost effective to administer A large amount of data can be collected in a short period of time	Participants cannot ask for clarification on instructions, unless survey is group-administered Participants may choose more than one response, skip items, or give invalid responses Open-ended responses may be grammatically incorrect and difficult to read Response rate may be low (if not group-administered) Difficult to follow up with those who have not completed or returned the survey
Interviews	To collect information in person or by telephone	Creation of interview script and recording form Trained interviewers Multiple contact attempts are often required to schedule the interview	Probing and clarification of answers is possible Interviewer has greater control over data collection	Potential interviewer bias Participants may give socially desirable answers Individuals may be difficult to contact

Focus Groups	To explore a topic in depth with a small group of participants	Trained moderator with facilitation skills Design of the session (i.e., strategy to be used) Moderator's guide with questions Multiple sessions may be required for different groups	Allows for in-depth discussion, clarification, and probing Participants interact and respond to others' ideas Underlying issues and unexpected outcomes may be revealed	Results are not representative Moderator may inadvertently introduce bias into the discussion One or two participants may dominate the discussion
Observation	To examine an object (an activity, process, behavior, performance, work sample, or product), record important features, and rate the object according to standards or criteria	Construction of observation form with instructions The object to be observed must be broken down into elements Trained observers and consistent use of the observation form Agreement among raters should be calculated	Objects that may be observed are diverse (e.g., behavior, work sample) Objects can be rated against standards or criteria Observation can be used to verify the findings of other evaluation tools	Potential observer bias Observation of individuals may affect their performance The observation may not represent a typical situation or product
Knowledge Assessments	To assess participants' knowledge in the learning or work environment	Construction of assessment Assessment must have content validity and must be reliable Must use exact test or an equivalent test for pre- and posttesting	Wide array of alternative formats: paper, scannable forms, computer-based-training embedded tests, email, and intra/Internet technology Easy to administer pre- and posttests Quickly scored, if technology is used	If a pretest is used, participants may score higher on the posttest because of familiarity (i.e., practice effect) Some participants may not perform optimally because of test anxiety

continued on page 102

Table 9-4. Common evaluation tools (continued).

Tool	Purpose	Requirements	Advantages	Disadvantages
Performance Assessments	To assess participants' skills in the learning or work environment	Construction of assessment with rating scales Skills to be performed must be broken down to the task level The criteria or standard of performance must be specified Assessment must have content validity and be reliable Necessary equipment and tools must be available	Variety of formats is available: paper, scannable forms, and interactive-multimedia embedded tests Provides direct evidence of skill	Potential rater bias Observation and rating may affect performance May not have time to measure all critical skills If a pretest is used, participants may score higher on the posttest due to familiarity (i.e., practice effect) Pretest may not be practical if time and business constraints exist
Key Business Metrics	To measure and track key business metrics over time	Metrics should be agreed upon by stakeholders Metrics should be aligned with organizational strategies and objectives, as well as the HPI intervention objectives Metrics should be sensitive to the effects of the intervention Metrics must be accurate, reliable, and timely	Manual and automated data collection is possible Frameworks, such as the balanced scorecard, may be used Benchmarking can be used to compare the relative performance of an organization within an industry	Global measures may not be meaningful in and of themselves Data capture may be inconsistent or biased Assumptions underlying data capture may be unknown

Table 9-5. Comparison of evaluation technologies.

Type of Technology	Ease of Use	Resources and Costs	Confidentiality
Paper-Based Optical Scanning	Most familiar survey or assessment form; optical scanning requires filling in bubbles	Duplication costs; expensive scannable forms and optical scanning technology	Depends on administration method (e.g., proctored or mailed)
Automated Telephone Polling	Asking and responding to complex questions is more difficult; limited number of response alternatives; limited length of surveys	Investment in specialized technology; telephone charges	Perceptions of confidentiality are enhanced because the participant initiates the call and uses an automated system
Fax	Same as paper-based survey or assessment except that it cannot be scanned	Costs include telephone charges and fax-on-demand PC functionality (sending capabilities)	May or may not be secure depending on location of sending and receiving fax machines; there may be concerns with linking to respondents' telephone numbers
Computer-Based-Training Diskette	Depends on ease of use and navigability of the survey or assessment	Cost of diskettes, design of embedded surveys or assessments, data extraction, possible mailing costs	Depends on return method (e.g., mailing)
Web-Based Technology	May be perceived to be difficult for those inexperienced with computers and the Internet	Cost is associated with software and vendor design and development costs	There may be concerns with company monitoring of intra/Internet activity
Email	Instructions may be necessary for those not familiar with email technology	Cost is associated with software	Concerns may exist about linking to respondents' email addresses

Kuhnert and McCauley, 1996

- automated telephone polling of managers on their use of an employee reward and incentive program
- skills-tracking program on the company's intranet for employees to self-assess and document their technical skills and competencies.

Technological alternatives should be chosen over paper-based forms if it is cost effective to do so. The use of technology cannot be justified if the only reason is to try the latest product or fad. Rather, the performance evaluator should compare options to determine the most appropriate technology for a given purpose. The factors to consider include those listed in table 9-5, the number of respondents, the familiarity of the respondents with technology, the anticipated return and completion rates, the timing associated with each option, and the potential for future use.

Techniques

There are three important techniques that the performance evaluator should consider prior to planning any data gathering related to an evaluation. Unfortunately, these techniques are somewhat technical and as such are often overlooked by inexperienced performance consultants. These techniques are evaluation design, sampling strategy, and tool quality.

The first technique, evaluation design, refers to the overall plan of data gathering for the evaluation, including timing and frequency of data gathering. The second technique, sampling strategy, refers to the number of individuals who will participate in the evaluation and the rationale for their participation. The third technique, tool quality, involves assessing the reliability and validity of evaluation tools before their use. The application of these techniques in an evaluation increases the reliability of the data and the sophistication of the data interpretation.

Evaluation Design

The purpose of planning the evaluation design is to increase the number of comparisons and interpretations that can be made from the evaluation data. Without a comparison based upon previous performance or the performance of another group, interpretations of the data will be limited to descriptive statements that are not very informative or useful.

Although there are many evaluation designs from which to choose, four are commonly used. A popular and relatively simple design is the one-group pre/post design. In this design, an evaluation tool, such as a performance assessment, is administered twice, once before the introduction of the HPI intervention—as a baseline measurement—and once after the intervention has been implemented. This enables the performance evaluator to determine whether there was an increase in performance due to the intervention. This design and others are described in table 9-6.

Another common design is the pre/post comparison group design. A group of employees from another work group is asked to participate in the evaluation in this design for the purpose of comparison. The evaluation tool

Table 9-6. Four common evaluation designs.

Evaluation Design	Description
One-Group Post Only	This design involves a single group of participants, an HPI intervention, and the use of at least one evaluation tool after the intervention is implemented. Because no comparison data is available, the data is primarily descriptive.
One-Group Pre/Post	The evaluation tool is administered twice in this design, once before the intervention has been introduced and once after implementation. This allows comparison of participants' performance at two points in time. This design has a practice effect, however, which means that participants may respond differently (e.g., score higher) on the second administration of the evaluation tool primarily because they are more familiar with the tool (and not because their performance actually increased).
Pre/Post Comparison Group	A comparison group of employees, who were not affected by the intervention, participates in the evaluation along with the group of employees who were directly affected by the intervention. So that the comparison will be valid, the comparison group should be similar to the intervention group in terms of professional position, level of skill, and other relevant characteristics.
Time Series	This design involves measuring the effects of HPI interventions over time. It is similar to the one-group pre/post design except that more than two tool administrations occur. The points of comparison are the multiple administrations of the evaluation tool. Again, practice effects cannot be ruled out.

is administered once before the intervention and again some time after the intervention has been in place. The comparison group should not be affected by the intervention although the group's performance is measured. This way, the performance of the two groups can be compared to determine whether the performance of the group that was affected by the intervention improved more than the performance of the comparison group.

To understand the importance of the design of the evaluation, it is helpful to examine some hypothetical evaluation data. The graphs in figure 9-1 show data from two different evaluation designs.

The first graph, which depicts data from a one-group post only design, includes one data point. This data point reflects the mean, or average, score that a group of employees achieved on a performance assessment. The percentage scores on the left side of the graph represent the assessment score, and the labels on the bottom of the graph represent when the assessment occurred. It is evident that the average score for employees was 75 percent in the first graph. In contrast, the second graph depicts data from a pre/post

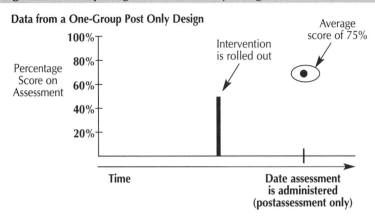

Figure 9-1. Comparing data obtained by using two evaluation designs.

Data from a One-Group Post Only Design

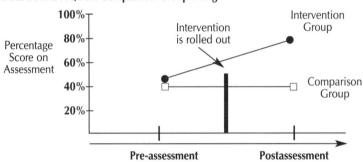

comparison group design. You will notice that this design yields four data points. On this graph, there are two points representing when the pre-assessment was administered and when the postassessment was administered. In this case, it is evident that the intervention group and the comparison group scored similarly on the pre-assessment. After the intervention was implemented, however, the performance of the intervention group increased, whereas the performance of the comparison group remained the same.

By comparing the four data points in the pre/post comparison group design, the performance evaluator is able to draw some conclusions that are not possible from the one-group post only design:

- Employees were generally performing at the same level prior to the intervention.
- The performance of employees who were affected by the intervention increased by 40 percentage points on the assessment.
- Those in the comparison group did not increase their performance over time, which suggests that a practice effect did not bias the data.
- It is likely that the performance of those exposed to the intervention improved because of the intervention and not because of some other factor.

From these interpretations, an assertion may also be made that other work groups in the business might also benefit from this intervention. These conclusions pertained to the average scores of the groups, but additional inferences might be drawn by examining individuals' scores.

As mentioned, the evaluation design is often overlooked in the interest of time. Inexperienced performance consultants may fear they are overreaching if they ask participants to complete more than one evaluation tool. Nevertheless, the benefit of using a sophisticated evaluation design is clear: more information for making judgments about the quality, value, and effectiveness of the HPI intervention! Furthermore, by using a sampling strategy— to be discussed next—all participants do not necessarily need to complete multiple evaluation tools.

Sampling Strategy

Sampling strategy refers to the number of individuals who will participate in an evaluation and the rationale for their participation. The sampling strategy is tied to the evaluation design in terms of when the groups will participate.

The performance evaluator can select from an array of sampling strategies. The most commonly used and the one discussed here is simple random sampling. In this procedure, a list of the entire population (all possible participants) is obtained and individuals are picked at random from the list. Everyone should have an equal chance of being selected. The easiest way to identify the participants is to pick a number between one and 10 and select, for example, every seventh individual on the list. The benefit conferred by random sampling is the elimination of potential bias in the selection process.

In some cases, you may want everyone affected by an intervention to participate in the evaluation. For example, if the group is small, it makes sense to include everyone. Perhaps the organization wants to offer all employees the opportunity to provide feedback and voice their concerns; in other words, a psychological benefit in terms of job satisfaction may be gained by including everyone despite the associated costs. Another rationale for including everyone in an evaluation may arise from organizational practices or policies, such as documentation of competencies or certification.

Furthermore, the sampling plan associated with the administration of any one evaluation tool may differ from the sampling plan for another tool. For example, a survey may be administered to all employees who are affected by an intervention whereas only a limited number of individuals may be randomly selected for direct observation of their performance. Whether you decide to use a sampling strategy or not, the rationale for the inclusion of particular groups should be clear and purpose-driven.

Tool Quality

The final technique that performance evaluators use is arguably the most important. It enables the performance evaluator to assess the reliability and validity of the selected evaluation tools. *Reliability* refers to the extent to which an evaluation tool consistently measures the same characteristic over time: Does the tool give the same results when the measurement is repeated?

Validity refers to the extent to which an evaluation tool measures what it is supposed to measure.

Consider the following reasons for assessing the reliability and validity of evaluation tools:

- An assessment may not be an accurate measure of the content and material that was covered during an instructional intervention.
- You cannot be certain that observers rated performers in a fair and consistent manner.
- You cannot be sure that interviewers conducted interviews in a neutral and consistent manner.

If you cannot rule out these sources of error, your ability to draw valid interpretations of the evaluation data will be limited. Assessing the reliability and validity of the evaluation tools provides a quality check before the tools are ever used. There are several techniques for calculating reliability and increasing validity.

Generally, reliability is easier to determine than validity. The different techniques for calculating reliability include test-retest reliability, equivalent forms reliability, split-half reliability, and inter-rater reliability. These are appropriate for use with knowledge and performance assessments, observations, and rating forms.

To calculate test-retest reliability, the same assessment is administered to a group of individuals twice with a period of time elapsing between the administrations. A correlation coefficient is calculated to determine the extent to which individuals' scores are related. Ideally, the scores on the first assessment will correlate highly with the scores on the second assessment. Alternatively, equivalent forms reliability can be used in a like manner. With this technique, two equivalent assessments must be designed. These two assessments should cover similar content, but the evaluation items or questions should be different; the level of difficulty of the items must be equal as well. By administering both assessments, the correlation between the assessments should be high. An alternative to these methods is split-half reliability. This technique involves the administration of only one assessment. The items on the assessment are randomly split into two halves with equivalent numbers of easy, moderate, and difficult items in each half. Individuals' scores on the one half of the assessment are correlated with their scores on the other half. This technique is useful when equivalent forms of an assessment are not available or if there is no opportunity for a second administration of the assessment.

To assess the reliability of observers, raters, or interviewers when multiple people have been involved in data collection, inter-rater reliability can be calculated. The purpose here is to rule out the possibility that a rater has inadvertently biased the data gathering. The same results should be obtained no matter which rater collects the data. To calculate inter-rater reliability, assign a code to each rater to associate participants' responses with raters. The participants' responses will vary, but no systematic difference should be associated with a particular rater. As an alternative, a simple percentage of agreement between raters can be calculated, although this percentage is not a true measure of reliability.

The validity of an evaluation tool is more difficult to assess. If a tool is not reliable, then certainly it will not be valid. However, a reliable tool still may not be valid; in other words, the tool may consistently measure some characteristic, but it may not be the characteristic that you intend to measure. Hence, the validity of evaluation tools must also be considered.

The different types of validity related to evaluation are face validity, content validity, concurrent validity, predictive validity, and construct validity (Trochim, 1999; Shrock and Coscarelli, 1989). Face validity refers to the extent to which a tool, such as an assessment, appears to the performer to be a test. For example, a performance assessment for cable installers would have high face validity to the performer if the questions on the assessment clearly relate to the activities involved in cable installation. Face validity is not an important parameter to measure, but if irrelevant items are included on an evaluation tool, participants may question the nature of these items and believe that the assessment is a waste of time.

Content validity is similar to face validity except that a subject matter expert performs an item analysis to judge whether the items on the assessment are valid for the purpose of the assessment. Content validation is commonly used and it does not involve a statistical calculation.

The most technical types of validity are concurrent validity, predictive validity, and construct validity. Concurrent validity refers to whether an assessment discriminates between master performers and nonmaster performers in an accurate manner. In contrast, predictive validity refers to how accurately a tool can predict future performance. Predictive validity is more relevant to HR selection systems and instruments than evaluation per se. Finally, construct validity refers to whether the items on a survey represent specific constructs of interest (job satisfaction or management effectiveness, for example); evaluation tools, however, are not generally analyzed with respect to construct validity.

Building the TEP on Solid Data

Conducting an HPI evaluation is much the same as carrying out scientific research: The results are only as good as the data. Step 4 of the TEP will help you be sure that you select and design the right evaluation tools, that you collect sufficient and sound data, and that the data can answer the targeted evaluation questions. The key is to plan ahead: Know the kind of data you need, select an appropriate tool and technological format, establish the reliability and validity of the tool, and develop an effective sampling strategy. Building a business case for any HPI intervention depends upon the hard data and results that you can present to management. By following step 4 of the TEP, your evaluation data will withstand scrutiny and demonstrate the quality, value, and effectiveness of the HPI intervention.

GATHERING AND ANALYZING DATA

"By the time you get to the analysis of your data, most of the really difficult work has been done. It's much more difficult to . . . develop a design structure. If you have done this work well, the analysis of the data is usually a fairly straightforward affair" (Trochim, 1999).

Strategic Questions Answered

Which statistical tests are commonly used to analyze evaluation data?

How do you determine which test to use?

What assumptions must be addressed when interpreting the data?

How do you make sense of multiple sources of data?

Which ethical challenges will the performance evaluator most likely encounter?

Gathering and analyzing evaluation data is the fifth step of the TEP. This step should be straightforward, because the groundwork was laid during step 4 of the TEP—designing the tools, technology, and techniques. The evaluation tools, technology, and techniques were selected and designed to answer the targeted evaluation questions. Hence, data gathering and analysis activities are driven by those tools, technology, and techniques. This chapter explains how to gather, prepare, analyze, and interpret evaluation data. Examples of ethical dilemmas associated with evaluation data are also presented in this chapter as something you must consider before you report your results.

Gathering and Preparing Data

The complexity of data gathering depends on the targeted evaluation questions and evaluation dimensions to be addressed, the number of evaluation tools used, the number of participant groups, and the sophistication of technology that is applied. Because a given evaluation typically involves multiple tools and participant groups, these activities should be project-managed to ensure that data gathering occurs as scheduled. In general, the performance evaluator oversees the following data gathering activities:

- coordinating the data gathering schedule
- monitoring data collection to ensure accuracy, completeness, and consistency
- coding the data manually if automated data collection technology was not used
- checking and cleaning the data
- organizing open-ended data by theme or category.

Evaluation data can be coded easily and entered into a standard spreadsheet application. The coding of participants' responses is based on the type of response alternative used with each item. As an example, we can examine an employee's rating of her manager's coaching skill on a survey (figure 10-1). The first item uses a yes/no response alternative, the second item is open-ended, the third item uses a five-point rating scale, and the fourth item uses the "check all that apply" response alternative.

Figure 10-1. Example survey of an employee's rating of her manager's coaching skills.

1. Have you received coaching from your manager in the past 30 days?

   ☑ **Yes**   ☐ **No**

2. Describe the coaching your manager provided to you:

   My manager reviewed a recent report I had written and gave me several suggestions on changes I could make to improve the report.

3. On the scale below, indicate how useful your manager's coaching was (circle the number):

   1 ---------------2---------------3--------------④--------------5
   Not Very   Extremely
   Useful   Useful

4. Check all of the following statements that are true:

   ☑ My manager is available to assist me when needed.

   ☑ My manager is willing to coach/assist.

   ☐ My manager encourages me to ask for assistance.

Because the respondent answered "yes" to item 1, enter a "1" in column B of the coding spreadsheet (figure 10-2). Typically lengthy open-ended responses are not coded; instead, they are included verbatim in a table. Hence, the respondent's answer to item 2 is not coded in the spreadsheet. For item 3, enter the number on the rating scale that the respondent circled ("4"). On the last item, the respondent endorsed the first and second statements but not the third. Response alternatives that allow the respondent to check all that apply are coded somewhat differently. Treat each of these statements as if they were separate survey items; the item numbers 4.1, 4.2, and 4.3 are used as labels to identify these items on the spreadsheet. A "1" is then assigned to each item that the respondent endorsed (items 4.1 and 4.2), and a "0" is assigned to the third item because the respondent did not endorse it. A codebook should be created with the response alternatives for each survey item and the coding schemes that were used.

Before any statistics are calculated, it is imperative to check and clean the data. Do this by printing the spreadsheet and systematically examining

Figure 10-2. Spreadsheet for coding responses to survey items in figure 10-1.

	A	B	C	D	E	F
	Survey on Managers' Coaching Skills					
1		Survey Items				
2	Respondents	Item 1	Item 3	Item 4.1	Item 4.2	Item 4.3
3	0001	1	4	1	1	0
4						
5						

Employees Survey / Managers Survey

the columns. When examining each column, consider the range of possible responses for each. For example, if item 1 employs the true/false response alternative, then the numbers in column B should be either "1" for true or "2" for false; if using this coding, any other numbers would be errors. Perform the same check on each column to verify the accuracy of the data.

If technology was used to capture evaluation data, manual coding may not be necessary. Many software programs are available to automate data coding and analysis. Alternatively, these statistical services may be contracted out to a vendor or consultant.

Analyzing Data

The evaluation data should be evaluated as soon as it becomes available. To do so, the performance evaluator relies upon basic statistical methods. The statistical tests that are commonly used to analyze evaluation data are identified in table 10-1.

Table 10-1. Common statistics used in evaluation.

Scales of measurement	
Examples of nominal, or categorical, data:	*Examples of interval, or scale, data:*
• Employee data (e.g., professional position)	• Survey items or interview questions with Likert-type rating scales
• Closed-ended survey items and interview questions (e.g., yes/no)	• Overall knowledge and performance assessment scores (e.g., 80 on a 100-point scale)
• Multiple choice items on knowledge assessments	
• Checklist items on performance assessments or observation forms	
Statistics	
• Frequency count	• Frequency count
• Percentage	• Percentage
• Cross-tabulation	• Cross-tabulation
• Mode	• Mean, Median, Mode
• Range	• Range
• Item analysis	• Cut-off scores
• Correlation	• Learning gain index
• Chi square test	• Correlation
	• Chi square test
	• *t*-test/analysis of variance (ANOVA)

Scales of Measurement

The first consideration when deciding which statistical test to use is the types of items and response alternatives on a given evaluation tool. The different response alternatives that were discussed in chapter 9 were open-ended, rating scale, multiple choice, binary, ranking, and checklist. Each of these types of response alternatives is associated with a specific scale of measurement. These scales of measurement are the nominal, ordinal, interval, and ratio scales (Hatcher and Stepanski, 1994).

The nominal scale is the simplest; this scale categorizes data into discrete categories. For example, a multiple choice question on an assessment uses the nominal scale of measurement because the respondent must select one of the mutually exclusive response alternatives. In other words, the respondent must select response *A, B, C, D,* or *E* and may choose only one of these.

The second scale of measurement is the ordinal scale. This scale is infrequently used for evaluating HPI interventions although it can be used for needs assessment purposes. The ordinal scale involves ranked or ordered data.

The third level of measurement is the interval scale; the distinguishing characteristic of the interval scale is the equal distance between data points on the scale. The five-point, Likert-type scale is an example of an interval scale because respondents assume there is an equal distance between neighboring numbers on the scale:

$$1 \text{----} 2 \text{----} 3 \text{----} 4 \text{----} 5$$

Although labels are used to anchor the numbers on the scale (i.e., to make the numbers on the scale meaningful), research has found that respondents focus on the numbers on the scale and assume equal distances between them (Chang, 1997). There is some debate surrounding this type of data, but it is general practice to consider data from Likert-type scales to be interval data. Another example of interval data is the total score on a knowledge or performance assessment. The final scale of measurement, the ratio scale, is rarely used for evaluation purposes.

Descriptive Statistics

Once you know the scales of measurement for your data, you can calculate simple, or descriptive, statistics. Frequency counts and percentages for each item are calculated as in the example in figure 10-3.

It is important to include the frequency count—the value of *n*, the number of individuals who responded to the item—so that the statistic is not misleading. Note that in this example the data has been analyzed and presented by region. The same can be done for business groups or departments within organizations or by other select demographic variables.

Measures of central tendency can be calculated next. These include the mean, median, and mode. The mean is the arithmetic average of a group of numbers. The median is the data midpoint—the point that divides the distribution of numbers in half when the data is arranged in ascending (or descending) order. The mode is the most frequently occurring number. The

Figure 10-3. Example calculations of frequency counts and percentages.

	Western Region		Central Region		Eastern Region		All Regions Combined	
Does the product matrix contain the information you need to sell the product?								
Yes	65.3%	n=45	78.4%	n=102	79.8%	n=87	76.3%	n=234
No	15.9%	n=11	15.4%	n=20	15.6%	n=17	15.4%	n=48
Respondent has not received the product matrix	18.8%	n=13	6.2%	n=8	4.6%	n=5	8.3%	n=26

mode is the only measure of central tendency that is calculated for nominal data; however, all three measures can be calculated for interval data. The range should also be noted for interval data. The range is a measure of the dispersion, or spread, of a group of scores arranged in ascending or descending order. For example, the experience of employees who participate in an HPI intervention may range from two months on the job to 60 months.

In addition to simple or descriptive statistics, item analysis, cutoff scores, and the learning gain index (LGI) can be calculated on assessments (Shrock and Coscarelli, 1989; Basarab and Root, 1992). Item analysis, which is performed during pilot-testing of the assessment, ensures that the assessment is aligned with the objectives of the intervention. Determining the cutoff score for passing an assessment enables the performance evaluator to distinguish between levels of performance to identify those who have mastered the objectives. The best measure of learning is the LGI (Basarab and Root, 1992). It is an index of learning that does not penalize those few learners who score high on the pre-assessment due to their existing knowledge.

Item analysis is performed at the pilot-test stage, with the resultant data analyzed as described here. Note that pre- and postassessments are pilot-tested at different times. For the pre-assessment item analysis, score each completed pre-assessment, and count the number of individuals who answered each item correctly. For example, if 12 of 18 individuals were able to answer item 1 correctly, record "12/18" for this item. This means that 67 percent of respondents were able to answer this item before they were exposed to the intervention; that is, they already possessed this knowledge. If many individuals were able to answer any item correctly, the item does not discriminate between individuals and, therefore, only a minimal amount of time should be spent on this content during the delivery of the intervention. Furthermore, this item may be omitted from the assessment. For the postassessment item analysis, score each completed postassessment in the same manner; however, this time count the number of individuals who answered each item incorrectly. If many individuals were unable to answer a particular item on the postassessment, the item may not be valid; that is, the item may not reflect the important learning to be gained as a result of the intervention. Alternatively, the content related to the learning may not have been covered adequately during the delivery of the intervention.

Two methods exist for establishing cutoff scores: the informed judgment method and the contrasting groups method. The informed judgment method involves establishing cutoff scores based on the advice of subject matter experts (SMEs) who examine each item on the assessment to determine whether a correct answer is required for mastery. The cutoff score is then calculated by summing the number of required items. For the contrasting groups method, a pilot test is conducted with two groups: master and non-master performers (Shrock and Coscarelli, 1989). By examining the means of the two groups, cutoff scores can be determined based on the difference between the means. All too often, an arbitrary "80 percent cutoff" is used as a rule of thumb instead of the systematic approaches presented here. Shrock and Coscarelli (1989) provide more information about establishing cutoff scores in the context of conducting assessments.

As mentioned, the best measure of learning is the LGI. The formula for calculating LGI is as follows:

$$\text{LGI} = \frac{(\text{Actual Postassessment}) - (\text{Actual Pre-Assessment})}{(\text{Maximum Postassessment}) - (\text{Actual Pre-Assessment})} \times 100$$

Table 10-2 shows training pre-assessment and postassessment scores of 14 individuals. The actual gain, potential gain, and learning gain indices are calculated from these pre- and postassessment scores.

The formula for calculating the LGI can be entered into a standard spreadsheet application for easy calculation. The potential gain refers to the maximum possible increase from pre-assessment to postassessment for a given person. This is calculated by subtracting an individual's pre-assessment from 100, for example:

$$100 - 25 = 75 \text{ potential gain}$$

The actual gain is the difference between an individual's pre-assessment and postassessment scores.

Inferential Statistics

The need for inferential statistics depends on the targeted evaluation questions, the evaluation dimensions, and the evaluation design. Not all data requires this level of statistical analysis. Simple or descriptive statistics, as well as open-ended questions that are categorized by themes, may be sufficient for evaluation purposes. Inferential statistics allow you to describe large amounts of data, draw conclusions based upon your data, establish the relia-

Table 10-2. Example calculations for learning gain index.

Course	Pre-Assessment	Postassessment	Actual Gain	Potential Gain	LGI
101	25.0	87.0	62.0	75.0	82.7
101	28.0	95.5	67.5	72.0	93.8
101	0.0	68.2	68.2	100.0	68.2
101	0.0	72.7	72.7	100.0	72.7
101	30.0	100.0	70.0	70.0	100.0
101	42.0	90.0	48.0	58.0	82.8
101	22.0	85.0	63.0	78.0	80.8
101	30.0	90.0	60.0	70.0	85.7
101	8.0	80.0	72.0	92.0	78.3
101	25.0	86.3	61.3	75.0	81.7
101	25.0	100.0	75.0	75.0	100.0
101	15.0	91.0	76.0	85.0	89.4
101	8.0	68.2	60.2	92.0	65.4
101	28.0	91.0	63.0	72.0	87.5

bility of your data through error estimation, and—most important—make statistical inferences based upon the data in your sample. A statistical inference is a decision, estimate, prediction, or generalization about a larger population based upon assessment of a limited-size sample, such as during pilot-testing of an intervention. By backing up your evaluation with statistical analysis, you can present a strong business case for (or against) an intervention, knowing that your data is reliable and that your inferences are sound.

Inferential statistics include the *t*-test, chi square, and analysis of variance (ANOVA) (Hatcher and Stepanski, 1994). Because these statistics are used with specific scales of measurement, there are assumptions to be met in using these statistics. For example, the chi square is appropriate for nominal data and is frequently used with surveys. In contrast, the *t*-test can be used with interval data to compare the difference between pre- and postassessment mean scores. Analysis of variance is another statistical procedure, similar to the *t*-test, which is used when three or more groups of performers are involved. Since additional assumptions are required of the data to appropriately apply inferential statistics, it is recommended that you consult a statistical reference when applying these statistics.

One additional group of statistics is used to determine the degree of association, or correlation, between two or more variables in an evaluation. Many different formulas are available for determining whether a correlation exists; again, the use of these formulas is dependent on the scales of measurement used on the evaluation tool.

Interpreting Data

Once the evaluation data is analyzed, the performance evaluator must interpret the data in a meaningful way. Before the performance evaluator can interpret the data, however, several important assumptions must be revisited. For example, the performance evaluator should consider the following:

- Were the evaluation tools valid and reliable?
- Was the sample representative of those who participated in the intervention?
- Was the data anomalous in any way?
- Were extreme scores evident?
- Was the data relatively complete without many missing responses?
- Is the data relatively free of bias (from interviewers, question wording, and so forth)?
- Is there any other reason to believe the data is not reliable?

Although many of these questions were addressed in early steps of the TEP, they are worth another look while interpreting the data. If the results are inconsistent with expectations (for example, performance did not improve), then these assumptions should be carefully examined to identify potential reasons.

In examining the data, the performance evaluator must make sense of the data as a whole. The data from different tools or sources should not be interpreted in isolation. In general, the data can be analyzed with respect to

- individual items (open- and closed-ended)
- comparisons to previously collected data or comparisons among work groups
- targeted evaluation questions
- evaluation dimensions
- relationships among evaluation dimensions.

Additional data should be sought to corroborate or refute your interpretations. Furthermore, additional data may be needed to substantiate interpretations. Indeed, the performance evaluator has a responsibility to interpret the evaluation data in a meaningful and ethical manner.

Ethical Challenges

Throughout the TEP, the performance evaluator will likely encounter ethical challenges or dilemmas. How do you know when you have encountered an ethical dilemma during the evaluation of a HPI intervention? P.A. Lawler (1998) suggests asking yourself the following questions:

1. Do I have a gut feeling that something is not right in this situation?
2. Will anyone be potentially harmed as a result of my decision, action, or inaction?
3. Is there a strong controversy regarding this decision?
4. Is this a decision that nobody else wants to make?
5. Will I feel hesitant in revealing my decision to others?

If you answered yes to any of these questions, you may indeed be facing an ethical dilemma. Some of the most common ethical dilemmas faced by performance evaluators are the misuse of evaluation data and the reporting of negative evaluation findings.

The pressure to use evaluation data for purposes other than those originally intended is an ethical dilemma that is encountered all too frequently. For example, a manager may pressure a performance evaluator to release individual-level data on specific employees when overall performance is low. In this case, professional codes of ethics state that individuals must be informed of the use of the data that is collected for evaluation purposes. If the evaluation team informed employees that the data would be analyzed and reported in aggregate form only, then it would be an ethical violation to release the individual-level data. The reason for analyzing and reporting data in aggregate form only is to encourage candor from evaluation participants and to increase participation in the evaluation process.

A second challenge concerns the misuse of evaluation data for HR planning and decision making. As another example, a manager may pressure a performance evaluator to use evaluation processes, including evaluation data, for performance appraisal of interventionists (trainer or instructional designer). The use of the evaluation data for performance appraisal in this case could result in the following problems:

- compromised validity of the evaluation findings because participants are reluctant to give low ratings to interventionists, leading to inflated ratings
- decreases in interventionists' morale, commitment, and participation in the evaluation
- an objection that evaluation participants are neither trained nor qualified to rate the performance of interventionists
- widespread feelings of vulnerability and suspicion surrounding the evaluation process.

A third ethical challenge concerns the reporting of negative evaluation findings. In this case, a performance evaluator may encounter pressure to omit negative findings from the evaluation report. This pressure may be in the form of assertions as to what should and should not be included in the report. One approach is to position these findings within the context of the organization by identifying those factors in the larger organization that may account for the success or failure of the intervention.

Performance evaluators clearly have an ethical responsibility to help stakeholders understand negative findings in this case. The findings may reveal that the intervention is not working as planned, has been mismanaged, or requires changes in design, among other things. These three examples represent only a few of the ethical challenges that you may encounter. When considering your course of action, it is helpful to identify alternative actions, consult with a respected colleague, and consult professional standards and codes of ethics to determine the best course of action. Contact the American Society for Training & Development, the International Society for Performance Improvement, the American Evaluation Association, or your own professional organization for specific information. In addition, your company or organization may have a business ethics department that has guidelines and consultants to assist you in such cases.

REPORTING RESULTS

"Success comes through communication and collaboration throughout the evaluation process and from the presentation of information in such a way that it is easily assimilated" (Torres, Preskill, and Piontek, 1996).

Strategic Questions Answered

How are evaluation results typically communicated to stakeholders?

What should be considered when making evaluation recommendations?

What does an evaluation report contain?

Why construct a communication matrix?

Communication with stakeholders is important throughout the TEP. Indeed, as Torres, Preskill, and Piontek (1996) assert, ongoing communication with stakeholders is critical to the success of an evaluation. Although stakeholders should be engaged throughout the evaluation process, they nonetheless anticipate the formal release of the evaluation results. As such, we have identified this process as the final step of the TEP. To ensure effective communication of the results, we discuss several different communication vehicles, including the classic evaluation report and formal presentations. Other vehicles that can communicate evaluation results are email alerts, intranet sites, and newsletters. Brochures, posters, and other marketing tools can also introduce new information across the organization.

When planning communication for various stakeholders, consider first the purpose of the communication in relation to each audience (Gelinas and James, 1998). In addition to the specific objectives of the communication, you will also want to assess each audience's needs. Several steps are involved in planning communications:

1. Identify your audience, and use matrices, such as the examples presented in figures 11-1 and 11-2, to help you plan communications.
2. Identify the purpose and goal of the communication for each audience in terms of specific objectives, audience needs, political sensitivities, content of the message, communication medium, timing, and sequencing for rollout.
3. Design and develop content and materials (email content, presentation packages, and so forth).
4. Prepare a master schedule of communication activities, including the timing and frequency of all communications.
5. Construct evaluation tools (feedback mechanisms) to assess the effectiveness of the communication.

Once the content of the communication (the message) has been identified and the content and materials are prepared, feedback mechanisms should be identified to later assess the effectiveness of the communication.

Figure 11-1. Example matrix for communication planning.

Audience	Objectives of the Communication	Audience Needs	Political Sensitivities	Content of the Message	Medium	Timing and Sequencing	Feedback Mechanism
Executives/ Business Owners							
Senior Managers							
Individuals Directly Affected by the Intervention							
Individuals Indirectly Affected by the Intervention							

125

Figure 11-2. Example matrix of audiences and communication media.

Audiences and Communication Medium	Executives/ Business Owners	Senior Managers	Individuals Directly Affected by the Intervention	Individuals Indirectly Affected by the Intervention
Formal presentation with break-out sessions	✓	✓	✓	
Presentation packages for managers to present at staff meetings		✓	✓	
Email message with hyperlink to Website of information			✓	✓

The Evaluation Report

The evaluation report is one of the major deliverables associated with evaluation. Stakeholders will be eagerly awaiting the report, which contains the results and recommendations. The evaluation report typically includes an executive summary, background information on the intervention, the purpose of the evaluation, the results, and recommendations (figure 11-3). Here are some suggestions for preparing the report:

- Use a conversational writing style so that the report is easy to read and understand.
- Use text boxes, bullets, headings, subheadings, and transitions to organize and simplify the material.
- Use visual aids—tables, charts, matrices, diagrams, and illustrations—to present the evaluation data in meaningful formats.
- Define acronyms and abbreviations on the first mention and include these in a glossary.
- Avoid using technical terms; if their use is necessary, they should be fully explained on the first mention and included in the glossary.

The evaluation strategy, including the evaluation tools used and data gathering schedule, should not appear in the body of the report. Instead, these technical details are included as appendices.

After the data has been presented and interpreted, stakeholders will expect your recommendations related to the intervention. When making recommendations, it is important to discuss several factors, including

- the anticipated effects of the recommendations or changes
- the timing associated with the changes
- the probability of successfully implementing the change
- any risks or barriers
- the cost of implementation
- the impact on staffing levels.

The benefits of the recommendations should always outweigh the costs of implementation; otherwise, the changes should not be recommended. In addition, the recommended changes should be compatible with the existing organizational structure, and the business owner should have control over the implementation (Torres, Preskill, and Piontek, 1996). To ensure that the recommendations are likely to be successful, they can be pilot-tested before widespread implementation.

Allow stakeholders sufficient time to review the report. To solicit feedback, distribute drafts to stakeholders in advance and schedule a formal group review. This opportunity to comment on the report, even while still in draft form, increases stakeholders' buy-in and ownership of the evaluation process and results.

Figure 11-3. Example table of contents for an evaluation report.

Formal Presentations

The evaluation report effectively summarizes the evaluation process and results, but different audiences will better understand and respond to the evaluation information if it is communicated via other vehicles, or media. Often the best vehicles for communication are presentations; these can consist of formal presentations to small or large stakeholder meetings, regular staff meetings, video- and audioconferences, and videotaped presentations.

Consider these questions as you design a formal presentation:

- What does this group of stakeholders need and want to know?

- What are the stakeholders' major concerns?
- What do they expect from this presentation?

Formal presentations can be structured as follows (Kramlinger, 1998; Scott and Jaffe, 1989):
1. Provide an explanation of the need for the change and how it came about.
2. Describe the change, what it means, and anticipated effects.
3. Explain how the change will affect this audience in particular.
4. Ask for questions.
5. Listen to feelings and respond appropriately.
6. Ask for help and support in making the change work.

Depending on the evaluation results and implications, employees may fear that change is imminent. For example, employees may wonder: "Will my job change?" "What will I gain or lose personally?" "Will my job performance be evaluated differently?" "Will I be rewarded differently?" The presenter should anticipate such concerns, and he or she should acknowledge that the concerns are understandable because employees may be reluctant to articulate their real concerns in a large group setting. In general, it is not a good idea to respond to emotion with logic or facts; it is better to positively respond to and acknowledge the audience's feelings and concerns.

It is useful to schedule formal executive presentations in conjunction with break-out sessions (Frady, 1997). Managers should lead the break-out sessions following the executive address.

Presentations may serve as informational sessions or as organizational interventions in themselves, depending on the design and intent of the communication. Table 11-1 lists some factors common to successful communication of evaluation results.

Table 11-1. Lessons learned about communication.

1. Select communication vehicles and design the content based on the purpose and objectives of the communication.
2. Pilot-test all communication vehicles for reaction to the message prior to general delivery.
3. Ensure that enablers (executive support) are aligned with communication efforts.
4. Rely on face-to-face communication more than any other vehicle; enlist multiple messengers in face-to-face communication to spread the word.
5. Plan to communicate repeatedly; remember that people require exposure to a consistent messages at least five to seven times before the message is internalized.
6. Assess the effect of the communication by gauging the audience's reaction to and its understanding of the message.
7. Address any disparities between communicated messages and managers' actions to clear up misunderstandings; explain the reasons for the disparities and make honest attempts to align behavior.

PROJECT-MANAGING THE TEP

"If we impress management or a client with insightful, data-driven performance analysis, then fail to deliver the performance improvement interventions in a reliable manner, we do little to further the human performance technology profession . . ." (Fuller, 1997).

Strategic Questions Answered

Why is a project-management framework necessary?

What activities and deliverables are associated with each step of the HPI process?

What are the critical responsibilities of the project manager?

As described in the introduction of this book, HPI is "a systemic and systematic approach to identifying the barriers that prevent people from achieving top performance" (Sugrue and Fuller, 1999), to solving performance problems, and to improving opportunities in the workplace. Human performance improvement involves five fundamental steps. Project-management activities associated with each step are listed in table 12-1. This chapter describes how the performance evaluator can apply a project-management framework to the TEP within the overarching HPI process. For more information about project-managing the overall HPI process, consult Fuller (1997).

A project-management framework is helpful to guide and organize the work to be performed as part of an evaluation and to determine whether the evaluation is on track for timely completion. Specific tasks, activities, deliverables, and timelines vary from evaluation to evaluation, but many activities are essential to every TEP. Those activities are the subject of this chapter, which will be particularly useful for the performance consultant serving the dual roles of performance evaluator and project manager of the HPI intervention.

Activities and Deliverables Associated with the HPI Intervention

The first step of the HPI process involves conducting a performance analysis to understand and validate the nature of the perceived performance problem. The performance consultant gathers data and information on the symptoms and frequency of the problem. The complexity of this particular step of the HPI process depends largely on the nature of the performance problem and the extent of data gathering that is required to fully understand the problem. Nonetheless, it is imperative that the specific details, tasks, activities, and deliverables associated with this step be reflected in your project plan.

Root-cause analysis identifies those factors that cause or contribute to the performance problem. The project manager is responsible for selecting an appropriate analytical method and conducting the analysis.

Once the performance and root-cause analyses have been reported to stakeholders and validated, the HPI intervention is selected and designed. The project manager should present multiple options to the stakeholder for solving the performance gap. For example, one or more interventions may be

Table 12-1. Project-managing the TEP within the HPI process.

HPI Phases	Activities and Deliverables at a Glance
Step 1: Performance Analysis	Partner and contract with the stakeholder Informally assess the perceived performance problem Conduct a formal assessment of the problem using multiple methods and tools Determine the current state of performance and validate with the stakeholder Construct a description of the desire state of performance Identify the performance gap to be resolved
Step 2: Root-Cause Analysis	Identify the factors that caused or contributed to the performance gap. Consider the following: • A lack of data, information, or consistent feedback • A lack of environmental support, resources, or tools • A lack of consequences, incentives, or rewards • Skills, knowledge, and attitudes • Motivation and expectations • Individual capacity
Step 3: Intervention Selection and Design	Review the performance and root-cause analysis data Select the most appropriate HPI intervention or combination of interventions (instructional and/or noninstructional) Provide options and recommendations to the stakeholder and secure project sponsorship Obtained the necessary resources (human, fiscal, time) Design and develop the intervention For large-scale initiatives, design change management and communication plans and align the intervention with related initiatives

continued on page 134

Table 12-1. Project-managing the TEP within the HPI process (continued).

HPI Phases	Activities and Deliverables at a Glance
Step 4: Implementation	Implement and monitor the intervention
	Ensure continued project sponsorship by the stakeholder
	Secure additional resources as necessary
Step 5: Evaluation (TEP)	Follow the six-step TEP*
	• Partnering with stakeholders
	• Understanding the intervention and organizational context
	• Targeting evaluation questions and identifying evaluation dimensions
	• Designing the tools, technology, and techniques
	• Gathering and analyzing data
	• Reporting results

*Refer to chapter 2 for a list of the activities and deliverables specifically associated with the TEP.

recommended or a combination of interventions may be required. Once the stakeholder has agreed on the solution to the performance gap (that is, the intervention) and has agreed to sponsor the project, the project manager secures the necessary resources and begins to design the intervention.

The next step of the HPI process is the most important—implementation. Carefully managing the rollout of the HPI intervention is critical. Yet, this step is often mismanaged (Fuller, 1997). The success or perceived success of an intervention depends on flawless execution. Preparing and implementing a change management and communication plan in accordance with the rollout is the key.

Ideally, the design of the evaluation should be planned prior to implementation of the intervention. The evaluation can, and should, be designed as the intervention itself is being designed. This way, the evaluation planning occurs much earlier in the HPI process. Unfortunately, evaluation is often conducted after the fact or post implementation. More often than not, evaluation activities are identified at the end of a project plan.

Activities and Deliverables Associated with the TEP

The TEP emphasizes partnering with stakeholders throughout the evaluation process. When planning and designing the evaluation, the performance evaluator meets with stakeholders to understand their needs and expectations related to the intervention and evaluation. Generally only one business owner sponsors, or contracts for, the evaluation, but all of the main players and stakeholders that are affected by the intervention should be involved in the process early on. Stakeholders play an important role in defining what the evaluation will and will not include. As conflicts arise due to differing needs, the performance evaluator should facilitate working sessions to gain consensus on the goals of the evaluation.

During the second step of the TEP, the performance evaluator gathers and reviews the original analysis and design documents on the intervention and begins interviewing program designers on the history and background of the intervention and any previous attempts at improving performance. The organizational context is also assessed at this time to understand the intervention within its system. If the evaluation is designed along with the intervention, there is no need to revisit this history.

The targeted evaluation questions and evaluation dimensions to be addressed are decided upon during the third step of the TEP, based on the scope and goals of the evaluation. At this point, the major evaluation activities, deliverables, and deadlines are agreed upon. The performance evaluator, serving in the role of project manager, must carefully manage all aspects of the evaluation: the construction and piloting of the evaluation tools to be used, the training of staff in tool administration procedures, and the scheduling of data gathering activities. Because most evaluations use several evaluation tools and multiple sources of data, the activities associated with these details should be carefully timed and sequenced. The schedule of data gathering activities can be relatively simple or complex depending on the complexity of the evaluation design.

The performance evaluator gathers and analyzes the evaluation data in the fifth step of the TEP. The important activities to track at this point include monitoring data collection, verifying data quality, data coding (if not automated), statistical analyses, and interpreting results. Because the data may be voluminous and because it emanates from many sources, the performance evaluator should track these activities on a project plan.

As the final step of the TEP, the performance evaluator reports and presents the results of the evaluation. After the evaluator releases the evaluation report, he or she will need to prepare and deliver a communication plan with presentation packages for different audiences. The need for presentation packages and, perhaps, other marketing materials should not be overlooked when initially agreeing to the evaluation deliverables; these are deliverables that stakeholders will eventually require to communicate the results of the evaluation effectively.

Other Responsibilities

In addition to tracking the activities and deliverables associated with the TEP, the performance evaluator assuming the role of project manager is responsible for

- creating a work breakdown structure of the tasks associated with activities
- delineating roles and responsibilities
- estimating realistic completion times for activities and deliverables
- scheduling tasks and activities, including meetings and working sessions
- managing human resources, contractors, and suppliers
- maintaining an action log or register
- securing technology, equipment, facilities, and materials
- ensuring effective communication (status reports, for example)
- monitoring quality throughout the TEP
- tracking each step of the TEP as a milestone
- identifying dependencies across activities
- analyzing the risks associated with actions and decision making
- planning for contingencies or alternative courses of action
- creating an escalation process to be used when roadblocks are encountered
- documenting lessons learned over the course of the project.

Carrying out a successful HPI project and TEP can be a daunting undertaking, but it can be simplified with a project-management framework to guide and organize the work to be performed and ensure that your project remains on track. Each project is a unique endeavor, but you can build a project plan based upon the list of activities and deliverables that are common to all HPI projects and the TEP.

Bringing the TEP Home to Your Organization

This book covered a great deal of terrain on the evaluation of HPI interventions. Make no mistake: One of the strongest messages for organizations in the new millennium is one of performance, measurement, and accountability. Likewise, the call for a new and better way to evaluate the quality, value, and effectiveness of HPI interventions has never been clearer. Toward this end, we have introduced a more flexible and meaningful approach to evaluation, one that

- is flexible enough to measure the wide variety of HPI interventions in use today
- takes into account the many variables and factors that enable and inhibit performance
- focuses on both the processes and outcomes of interventions
- provides information for decision making
- ensures stakeholder return-on-expectations.

Question-and-Answer Session

We now conclude with some answers to questions about the targeted evaluation process that are likely to arise as you apply the process in your organization.

Our organization is comfortable with Kirkpatrick's four-level model of training evaluation. We have been using it for years. Why should we adopt the TEP?

We have no simple answer for this one. Most HPI professionals are as predisposed to Kirkpatrick's model as organizations are to training as an intervention for solving all performance problems. Our recommendation is an incremental approach to implementing the TEP. Introduce the TEP as a flexible approach to evaluation that will allow you to generate meaningful evaluation questions and identify relevant processes, factors, and outcomes related to the intervention. Use the targeted evaluation questions and evaluation dimensions presented in chapters 4–8 as a starting point.

Whatever you do, avoid harsh criticism of the existing evaluation process in your organization because you will alienate stakeholders and increase resistance to implementing the TEP in your organization.

Why bother assessing the organizational context?

It is important to assess the organizational context in which the intervention is embedded because factors in the larger organization may ultimately account for the success or failure of the intervention. Assessing the organizational context need not be a complex, lengthy process, however. You can conduct this assessment informally with stakeholders.

Do not embark on a mission to uncover all of your organization's problems and ills while you are assessing the organizational context. Remember that you are only identifying and documenting potential barriers to the success of the HPI intervention.

Can we generate the targeted evaluation questions ourselves rather than involving stakeholders in working sessions?

Yes, after reading this book, you should be more than capable of generating targeted evaluation questions. To ensure stakeholder return-on-expectation, however, it is important to involve as many stakeholders as possible in the decision about which questions to answer. If it is not possible for stakeholders to attend on-site working sessions, be flexible. Keep them abreast of the targeted evaluation questions that the team is considering through alternative means of communication. The important point is to actively engage stakeholders in the process to ensure their buy-in to the evaluation questions.

Do not exclude powerful or vocal stakeholders from the TEP.

Why not use all the evaluation dimensions?

The evaluation dimensions presented in this book are merely examples of processes, factors, and outcomes that may be important to evaluate. The evaluation dimensions that are ultimately selected depend on stakeholder interests and informational needs and available resources. Another important consideration is whether stakeholders are willing to implement change with respect to a given evaluation dimension.

Do not waste valuable resources measuring factors, processes, and outcomes that stakeholders are not willing to change.

Which is more important to evaluate: processes, factors (intervening variables), or outcomes?

Many would argue that bottom-line results (outcomes) are what matters most. When the anticipated bottom-line results are not achieved, it is likely the result of a faulty implementation process or an intervening variable or factor. If this data is not gathered as part of the evaluation endeavor, it will be difficult, perhaps impossible, to identify the root cause. Therefore, it is critical to consider the relevant processes and intervening variables that enable and inhibit performance in the workplace.

 Do not be short-sighted by evaluating outcomes only.

Are some evaluation tools better than others?

Many performance consultants are biased toward the use of one evaluation tool over another. The traditional Kirkpatrick model has perpetuated the belief that outcomes are best measured by specific tools. For example, that on-the-job performance is best measured through direct observation or that surveys are only to be used for measuring learner satisfaction. In reality, there are many different ways to measure the same thing. Rather than using a pre-determined tool, the performance evaluator should attempt to answer the targeted evaluation questions with multiple evaluation tools and sources.

 Do not use a tool that stakeholders believe lacks validity and credibility.

The Test

The TEP is vital to the ongoing cycle of improving performance in the workplace, and, most important, the TEP provides results that performance evaluators and stakeholders can trust. We have applied the TEP in our organizations and been encouraged by the results, but our idea for evaluation must weather the test of time through practice and action. The approach is flexible enough to apply to myriad HPI interventions in a broad spectrum of organizations. We invite you to apply the TEP in your organization and share your results with us.

GLOSSARY

Action Planning: A transfer of training strategy involving the planning of specific actions that the learner intends to take to apply the newly acquired skills on the job. An evaluation dimension related to the evaluation of training with respect to training transfer.

Actual State: The current or actual level of performance (e.g., what people are currently able to do).

Ad Hoc: An activity for a special case or specific purpose that occurs after the fact.

Aggregate Data: Data representing more than one observation or more than one individual (e.g., an average test score across all participants).

Analysis of Variance (ANOVA): An inferential statistic used to determine whether differences between two or more group means are statistically significant. Fundamentally similar to the *t*-test but typically used for three or more groups.

Benchmarking: An approach to process improvement that involves studying best-in-class organizations to understand and adopt their practices and processes; involves more than the comparative analysis of business metrics.

Business Owner/Sponsor: A powerful stakeholder who can authorize and provide resources for the successful implementation of HPI interventions and related activities. Typically at the executive level.

Certification: To attest that a program, product, process, or person satisfies some criterion (i.e., a predetermined standard). An evaluation dimension related to the evaluation of training and on-the-job training.

Chi Square: A statistical significance test used for variables that have been organized into categories and contingency tables (e.g., cross-tabulations of survey data and demographic information).

Closed-Ended: A type of response alternative that is limited to listed alternatives (e.g., yes or no, true or false).

Coaching: A noninstructional intervention involving ongoing guidance, instruction, and feedback to improve work performance and competency. Synonymous with mentoring although this term generally refers to a more formal relationship between a mentor and protégé.

Coding: The process whereby raw data is translated into numerical values for tabulation and statistical analysis.

Competency: A cluster of related knowledge, attitudes, and skills that affect a major part of an employee's job. An evaluation dimension related to the evaluation of instructional interventions (e.g., training, on-the-job training).

Computer-Based Training (CBT): Instruction provided through computer technology.

Continuous Improvement: An approach to organizational improvement that is conducted on an ongoing basis; this approach is similar to process redesign, however, it is not limited to the improvement of processes.

Contracting: A critical first step in most consultation approaches involving the initial planning of a project (e.g., identification of stakeholders' informational needs, expectations, priorities, and deliverables).

Core Process: A major process that is vital to the business; typically spans two or more organizational functions.

Cultural Change: A large-scale initiative aimed at changing the underlying values, beliefs, and norms that guide individual, group, and organizational behavior.

Customer: External and internal individuals to whom products or services are delivered.

Customer Capital: A category of intellectual capital that includes customer information such as purchasing patterns, financial stability, customer satisfaction, loyalty to products, and information about the market. Also an evaluation dimension related to knowledge management.

Cutoff Score: A minimum standard for passing some form of assessment or test (i.e., a score that separates master performers from non-master performers).

Decision point: A point in the process where a decision must be made.

Demographic Items: Questions that pertain to personal characteristics, work history, and prior HPI intervention experience (e.g., gender, professional position, prior training experiences).

Descriptive Statistics: Statistics used to organize, summarize, and describe data and information from a set or sample of observations.

Desired State: The future or desired level of performance (e.g., what people should be able to do).

Electronic Performance Support Systems (EPSS): A noninstructional intervention that provides online help or expert advice through a user-friendly computer interface.

Elimination of Barriers/Task Interference: A noninstructional intervention that involves removing barriers impeding worker's optimal performance on the job.

Evaluation: The systematic process of gathering and analyzing data and other objective information on HPI processes and outcomes within the context of the business or organizational setting to determine the quality, value, and effectiveness of the intervention.

Evaluation Design: The strategy used in collecting evaluation data (e.g., tools, timing, and frequency of data collection).

Evaluation Dimension: All relevant factors, processes, or outcomes associated with particular types of HPI interventions; an area within the context of an intervention that is the focus of an evaluation.

Evaluation Utilization: The effective use of evaluation results for decision making.

Expert System: A type of EPSS; a specialized, decision-support system that assists users with diagnosis and troubleshooting activities.

Explicit Knowledge: Formal knowledge that is easily shared and articulated; this type of knowledge can be quantified more readily than tacit knowledge. Also, an evaluation dimension related to knowledge management.

Feedback Systems: A noninstructional intervention that provides workers with corrective feedback on the nature of their performance to improve performance.

Focus Group: A tool or method used to explore a topic in depth with a small group of participants.

Frequency Count: A description of the number of times an attribute is observed.

Front-End Analysis: The first stage of the instructional systems design and development process; involves systematic data collection. Generally includes a needs assessment, performance analysis, and task analysis.

Gap: The difference between the desired state and actual state. Frequently referred to as the performance gap or problem.

Help System: A type of EPSS; a system that provides online help, advice, and demonstrations to the user.

Human Capital: A category of intellectual capital that is associated with employees' knowledge, skill, competency, and innovation; includes the organization's culture, values, and philosophy. Also an evaluation dimension related to knowledge management.

Human Performance Improvement (HPI): "A systemic and systematic approach to identifying the barriers that prevent people from achieving top performance" (Sugrue and Fuller, 1999), to solving performance problems, and to improving opportunities in the workplace. Generally synonymous with human performance technology (HPT), performance improvement, performance technology, and performance consulting.

Inferential Statistics: Statistics that allow evaluators to generalize their findings or results from the sample of individuals on which they have collected data to a larger population or group.

Infobase: An electronic knowledge base or database that contains relevant information employees need to perform their jobs (Gery, 1991).

Input: The materials, equipment, information, and resources that are needed to carry out a business process.

Instructional Delivery: The presentation of course content and material; the facilitation of structured learning activities.

Instructional Design: A systematic process for determining the instructional content and learning objectives, sequencing information and materials, and selecting the methods and media to be used. An evaluation dimension related to the evaluation of instructional interventions.

Instructional Intervention: HPI interventions of an instructional or learning nature (e.g., training, on-the-job training).

Intellectual Capital: Knowledge that is of value to an organization; includes human capital, structural capital, and customer capital. Also an evaluation dimension related to knowledge management.

Interval: A level of measurement or a scale describing variables according to some attribute that also establishes equal interval (e.g., Likert-type scale).

Intervention Selection and Design: The process of selecting and designing an appropriate intervention; a step of the HPI process.

Interview: A tool or method used to collect information in person or by telephone.

Item Analysis: A statistical evaluation of the quality of a newly constructed test or assessment (e.g., identifying problematic test items, assessing test difficulty, assessing the extent to which the items align with the objectives and content of the intervention, determining content validity).

Items: The questions or statements to be answered on surveys and assessments, or in interviews.

Job Aid: A noninstructional intervention designed to provide information, to prompt procedures, or to make answers readily available to workers as an immediate reference within the work environment; sometimes referred to as a work or performance aid.

Job Design/Redesign: A noninstructional intervention involving the creation or redesign of jobs to make them more enriching and meaningful to increase worker motivation and performance.

Key Business Metric: An important business indicator that is tracked and reported over time (e.g., accuracy metrics, quality metrics, customer satisfaction metrics, and so forth).

Knowledge Assessment: A tool or method used to assess participants' knowledge in the learning or work environment.

Knowledge Management: The process by which intellectual capital is captured, managed, and leveraged across an organization (e.g., documenting, tracking, and leveraging individuals' talent and expertise across the organization).

Knowledge Repositories: A central place where knowledge and information is stored (e.g., in databases, on intranets) for employees to retrieve. An evaluation dimension related to knowledge management.

Knowledge Transfer: The formal process of sharing and using knowledge across the organization through human interaction; knowledge transfer may be facilitated by the use of technology. Also an evaluation dimension related to knowledge management.

Learning: The process of acquiring knowledge and skill; a change in perceptions, attitudes, and behaviors of individuals, groups, and organizations. An evaluation dimension related to the evaluation of instructional interventions and some noninstructional interventions.

Learner Characteristics: The individual attributes that affect the effectiveness of an HPI intervention (e.g., personality, self-confidence, motivation, achievement orientation, attention span). An evaluation dimension related to the evaluation of instructional interventions.

Learning Gain Index: An accurate pre- and postassessment measure of learning; does not penalize learners who score relatively high on the pre-assessment.

Likert-Type Scale: A popular response alternative developed by Rensis Likert; includes a range of possible closed-ended responses (e.g., strongly agree, agree, disagree, strongly disagree).

Measures of Association: Statistics that describe the way two variables relate to one another (e.g., correlation, regression, multiple regression).

Measures of Central Tendency: Statistics that describe a set of individual scores with a single index (mean, median, and mode).

Measures of Variability: Statistics that describe the dispersion of scores within a distribution (e.g., variance, standard deviation, quartile deviation).

Mentoring Relationship: An informal relationship between a mentor and protégé involving ongoing guidance, instruction, and feedback; more personal than coaching.

Meta-Evaluation: The process of evaluating the evaluation; includes lessons learned and continuous improvement.

Needs Assessment: A generic term referring to the assessment of stakeholder needs; involves systematic data collection.

Nominal: A level of measurement or scale describing variables that are placed into categories that differ qualitatively from one another but not on a quantitative dimension (e.g., gender, political affiliation, ethnicity, occupation). Demographic information is usually nominal level data.

Noninstructional/Learning Intervention: HPI interventions of a noninstructional nature (e.g., job aids, EPSS, process improvement, process redesign).

Observation: A tool or method used to examine an activity, process, behavior, performance, work sample or product to record key features and rate the object according to predetermined criteria.

On-the-Job Learning: The process of acquiring knowledge and skill in the work environment. An evaluation dimension related to the evaluation of OJT.

On-the-Job Training (OJT): A structured instructional intervention designed to facilitate knowledge and skill mastery in the work environment.

On-the-Job Training (OJT) Delivery: The presentation of OJT content and material and facilitation of structured learning activities. An evaluation dimension related to the evaluation of OJT.

On-the-Job Training (OJT) Design: A systematic process for determining OJT content and learning objectives, sequencing information and materials, and selecting the methods and media to be used. An evaluation dimension related to the evaluation of OJT.

On-the-Job Training (OJT) Trainer Effectiveness: The extent to which an OJT trainer applies sound adult learning principles, presents the content and materials consistently as designed, and promotes a learning environment conducive to learning. An evaluation dimension related to the evaluation of OJT.

Open-Ended: A type of response alternative that allows the respondent to generate the answer on his or her own; lines or spaces often follow the item, allowing respondents to write their answer.

Ordinal: A level of measurement or scale describing variables that are ranked or ordered with respect to their possession of some attribute from highest to lowest.

Organization Design/Redesign: A noninstructional intervention involving the establishment and maintenance of the allocation of work duties and reporting relationships.

Organization Development (OD): The application of strategies for improving intra- and intergroup relationships within organization; a process by which behavioral science knowledge and practice are used to help organizations achieve greater effectiveness.

Organizational Context: Important factors to consider in designing the evaluation (e.g., mission and strategy, business performance goals, and so forth). An evaluation dimension related to all HPI interventions. Also, a component of step 2 of the targeted evaluation process.

Organizational Culture: The underlying value, beliefs, and norms that guide individual, group, and organizational behavior.

Organizational Learning: The intentional use of learning processes at the individual, group, and systems levels to continuously transform the organization in a direction that is increasingly satisfying to stakeholders (Dixon, 1994). It involves learning from past successes and failures, critical thinking, risk taking, innovating, and exchanging ideas throughout the organization. Also an evaluation dimension related to knowledge management.

Organizational Results: The overall effect of an HPI intervention on the organization. An evaluation dimension related to the evaluation of all HPI interventions.

Output: The products or services that are created by a business process and passed on to the customer.

Performance Analysis: A formal analysis to identify, understand, and validate the nature of the perceived performance problem or improvement opportunity.

Performance Appraisal: A formal evaluation of employee performance and behaviors with respect to a role or job function during a specified time period. An evaluation dimension related to reward and incentive systems.

Performance Assessment: A tool or method used to assess participants' skills in the learning or work environment.

Performance Expectations: A noninstructional intervention that involves establishing specific, measurable, and attainable performance expectations or objectives.

Performance Gap: The difference between the desired state and actual state. Sometimes referred to as the gap or problem.

Pilot Test: A trial run that provides information to improve or revise a product (e.g., data collection tool) or process.

Positive Reinforcement: A consequence that positively affects employee behavior. Involves encouraging employees to increase their performance through praise and appreciation of effort. An evaluation dimension related to reward and incentive systems.

Practice Effect: An unanticipated effect that occurs when a test is administered twice, the results of which indicate improved performance even if no intervention has occurred between the two assessments.

Prerequisites: The skills and knowledge required before participating in an instructional intervention. An evaluation dimension related to the evaluation of instructional interventions.

Probe: A statement used by an interviewer to clarify a response; examples are: "Tell me more about that" and "Anything more?"

Process: A series of sequential activities, tasks, or steps that transforms inputs from suppliers into outputs for customers.

Process Design: An approach to creating, or designing, new business processes that previously did not exist.

Process Improvement: A method used to improve business processes through process redesign, benchmarking, reengineering, or continuous improvement; also termed business process improvement.

Process Redesign: An approach to redesigning existing business processes for incremental improvement.

Process Reengineering: The radical redesign of business processes for dramatic improvement.

Project Management: A set of principles, methods, tools, and techniques for effective management of objective-oriented work; it provides support for both the goal of producing an end product and for the enabling processes of planning, change management, control, and preventive and corrective action (Fuller, 1997).

Random Selection: A technique for selecting individuals or elements to participate in a given evaluation; it means that each participant or element in a population has the same chance or probability of being selected.

Ratio: A level of measurement or scale describing variables that have ordinal and interval properties that also possess a true or absolute zero.

Recruitment: Those practices and activities carried out by an organization with the primary purpose of identifying and attracting potential employees. An evaluation dimension related to reward and incentive systems and telework.

Response Alternatives: The options for answering a question; broad categories include open- and closed-ended response alternatives.

Reward and Incentive System: A system designed to attract and retain employees. Reward and incentive systems compensate, encourage, and reinforce employees for their performance on the job.

Root-Cause Analysis: An analysis to identify underlying factors that cause or contribute to the perceived performance gap or problem (i.e., symptoms).

Sampling: A method used to decide on the characteristics and size of the group(s) of individuals who will participate in an evaluation.

Self-Paced Instruction: An instructional intervention that enables the learner to acquire knowledge and skills at his or her own pace without the direction of an instructor or facilitator.

SMART: The acronym SMART stands for the key characteristics required to provide effective rewards and incentives. Rewards should be Specific, Meaningful, Achievable, Reliable, and Timely. An evaluation dimension related to reward and incentive systems.

Solution: The HPI intervention(s) chosen to address the identified performance gap or problem.

Stakeholder: Anyone interested in or affected by an HPI intervention, including business owners/sponsors, senior managers, front-line clients, employees, and HPI staff.

Standardization of Procedures: Work-related procedures that are performed consistently irrespective of circumstances. An evaluation dimension related to job aids.

Structural Capital: A category of intellectual capital that includes hardware, software, databases, organizational structure, business processes, patents, trademarks, and copyrights that are owned by the organization. An evaluation dimension related to knowledge management.

Sub-Process: Part of a core process that is designed to accomplish a specific objective.

Supplier: External and internal individuals who provide inputs to the process.

Survey: A tool or method used to collect information from many respondents through paper-based or technological means.

Tacit Knowledge: Informal knowledge, based on intuition, values, beliefs, and experience, which is difficult to articulate and communicate to others. An evaluation dimension related to knowledge management.

Talent Retention: The retention of highly skilled and valued employees. An evaluation dimension related to reward and incentive systems and telework.

Targeted Evaluation Questions: Evaluation questions that are specific and focused and lend themselves to measurement.

Team Rewards: Rewarding group members for their contribution to team accomplishments. An evaluation dimension related to reward and incentive systems.

Telemanagement: The management of teleworkers or virtual teams who do not work in the same location as the manager. An evaluation dimension related to telework.

Telework Environment: Any designated setting in which telework is performed; it may be home-based or a telework center. A telework environment should have the following: adequate work space; access to telephone and electrical outlets; security and safety of documents and equipment; noise, temperature, and light control; and separation from any ongoing domestic activities. An evaluation dimension related to telework.

Train-the-OJT-Trainer: The process of providing formal instruction to OJT trainers. An evaluation dimension related to the evaluation of OJT.

Trainer Effectiveness: The extent to which a trainer applies sound, adult-learning principles, presents the content and materials consistently as designed, and promotes a learning environment conducive to learning. An evaluation dimension related to the evaluation of training.

Training Aid: An instructional intervention that provides information to support the knowledge and skills acquired in the training environment.

Training Delivery: The presentation of training content and materials. Training delivery methods include leader or instructor-led training in the classroom, video-based instruction, CBT, intranet/Internet-based training, distance learning, and OJT. An evaluation dimension related to the evaluation of training.

Training Environment: Any setting in which training is performed. An evaluation dimension related to the evaluation of training.

Training Relevancy: The applicability and usefulness of the training content to the learners' respective job or role. An evaluation dimension related to the evaluation of training.

Transfer Climate: The combined effect of learner characteristics and overall work environment on the extent that training transfers to the job. A positive organizational transfer climate increases the likelihood that the learner will demonstrate transfer behavior (apply newly acquired skills to the job). An evaluation dimension related to the evaluation of training.

Transfer of Training: The learner's application of the knowledge and skills acquired in training to the job immediately following training. An evaluation dimension related to the evaluation of training.

Trigger: A point in the process that signals the initiation of a simultaneous process.

_t_-Test: An inferential statistic used to determine whether the difference between two group means is statistically significant.

Work Environment: Any designated setting in which work is performed. An evaluation dimension related to the evaluation of training or other HPI interventions.

REFERENCES

Alliger, G.M., and E.A. Janak. (1989). "Kirkpatrick's Levels of Training Criteria: Thirty Years Later." *Personnel Psychology, 42,* 331–340.

Baldwin, T.T., and J.K. Ford. (1988). "Transfer of Training: A Review and Directions for Research." *Personnel Psychology, 41,* 63–105.

Basarab, D.J., and D.K. Root. (1992). *The Training Evaluation Process.* Boston: Kluwer Academic Publishers.

Bassi, L.S. (1997). "Harnessing the Power of Intellectual Capital." *Training & Development, 51*(12), 25–30.

Bassi, L., S. Cheney, and E. Lewis. (1998). "Trends in Workplace Learning: Supply and Demand in Interesting Times." *Training & Development, 52*(11), 51–75.

Bates, R.A. (1999). "Measuring Performance Improvement." *Advances in Developing Human Resources, 1,* 47–67.

Berardinelli, P., J. Burrow, and L. Dillon-Jones. (1995). "Management Training: An Impact Theory." *Human Resource Development Quarterly, 6*(1), 79–90.

Bernthal, P.R. (1995). "Evaluation That Goes the Distance." *Training & Development, 49*(9), 41–45.

Boyett, J.H., and J.T. Boyett. (1998). *The Guru Guide: The Best Ideas of the Top Management Thinkers.* New York: John Wiley & Sons.

Broad, M.L., and J.W. Newstrom. (1992). *Transfer of Training.* Reading, MA: Addison-Wesley Publishing.

Chang, L. (1997, October). "Dependability of Anchoring Labels of Likert-type Scales." *Educational and Psychological Measurement, 57*(5), 800–807.

Chelimsky, E., and W.R. Shadish, editors. (1997). *Evaluation for the 21st Century: A Handbook.* Newbury Park, CA: Sage Publications.

Cherniss, C., and M. Adler. (2000). *Promoting Emotional Intelligence in Organizations: Guidelines for Practitioners.* Alexandria, VA: American Society for Training & Development.

Cohen, S. (1997). "On Becoming Virtual." *Training & Development, 51*(5), 30–37.

Cummings, T.G., and C.G. Worley. (1993). *Organization Development and Change* (5th edition). New York: West Publishing Company.

Davenport, T.H., and L. Prusak. (1998). *Working Knowledge: How Organizations Manage What They Know.* Boston: Harvard Business School Press.

Davis, J.R., and A.B. Davis. (1998). *Effective Training Strategies: A Comprehensive Guide to Maximizing Learning in Organizations.* San Francisco: Berrett-Koehler Publishers.

Dean, P., and D. Ripley. (1997). *Performance Improvement Pathfinders: Models for Organizational Learning Systems* (volume one). Washington, DC: International Society for Performance Improvement.

Dean, P., and D. Ripley. (1998a). *Performance Improvement Interventions: Instructional Design & Training* (volume two). Washington, DC: International Society for Performance Improvement.

Dean, P., and D. Ripley. (1998b). *Performance Improvement Interventions: Performance Technologies in the Workplace* (volume three). Washington, DC: International Society for Performance Improvement.

Dean, P., and D. Ripley. (1998c). *Performance Improvement Interventions: Culture and Systems Change* (volume four). Washington, DC: International Society for Performance Improvement.

Dixon, N. (1994). *The Organizational Learning Cycle: How We Can Learn Collectively.* New York: McGraw-Hill.

Edvinsson, L., and M.S. Malone. (1997). *Intellectual Capital: Realizing Your Company's True Value By Finding Its Hidden Brainpower.* New York: Harper Business.

Fisher, K., and M.D. Fisher. (1998). *The Distributed Mind: Achieving High Performance Through the Collective Intelligence of Knowledge Work Teams.* New York: AMA-COM.

Fishman, C. (1998, August). "The War for Talent." *Fast Company: How Smart Businesses Work,* 104–108.

Fowler, F.J. (1993). *Survey Research Methods* (2d edition). Newbury Park, CA: Sage Publications.

Foxon, M. (1997). "The Influence of Motivation to Transfer, Action Planning, and Manager Support on the Transfer Process." *Performance Improvement Quarterly, 10*(2), 42–63.

Frady, M. (1997). "Get Personal to Communicate Coming Change." *Performance Improvement, 36*(7), 32–33.

Fuller, J. (1997). *Managing Performance Improvement Projects: Preparing, Planning, and Implementing.* San Francisco: Pfeiffer.

Gelinas, M.V., and R.G. James. (1998). *Collaborative Change: Improving Organizational Performance.* San Francisco: Pfeiffer.

Gery, G.J. (1991). *Electronic Performance Support Systems: How and Why to Remake the Workplace Through the Strategic Application of Technology.* Cambridge, MA: Ziff Communications Company.

Gilbert, T.F. (1992). "Forward." In *Handbook of Human Performance Technology: A Comprehensive Guide for Analyzing and Solving Performance Problems in Organizations,* H.D. Stolovitch & E.J. Keeps, editors. San Francisco: Jossey-Bass.

Hackett, B. (1997). *The Value of Training in the Era of Intellectual Capital: A Research Report* (1199-97-RR). New York: The Conference Board.

Hamblin, A.C. (1974). *Evaluation and Control of Training.* London: McGraw-Hill.

Harless, J.H. (1989). *Job Aid Analysis, Design, and Development.* Newnan, GA: Harless Performance Guild.

Harrington, H.J. (1991). *Business Process Improvement: The Breakthrough Strategy for Total Quality, Productivity, and Competitiveness.* New York: McGraw-Hill.

Harrington, H.J., E.K. Esseling, and H.V Nimwegen. (1997). *Business Process Improvement Workbook: Documentation, Analysis, Design, and Management of Business Process Improvement.* New York: McGraw-Hill.

Hatcher, L., and E.J. Stepanski. (1994). *A Step-by-Step Approach to Using the SAS System for Univariate and Multivariate Statistics.* Cary, NC: SAS Institute Inc.

Heneman, R.L., and M.T. Gresham. (1998). "Performance-Based Pay Plans." In *Performance Appraisal: State of the Art in Practice,* J.W. Smither, editor. San Francisco, Jossey-Bass.

Holton III, E.F. (1996). "The Flawed Four-Level Evaluation Model." *Human Resource Development Quarterly, 7*(1), 5–29.

Holton III, E.F. (1999). "Performance Domains and Their Boundaries." *Advances in Developing Human Resources, 1,* 26–46.

Holton III, E.F., R.A. Bates, D.L. Seyler, and M.B. Carvalho. (1997). "Toward Construct Validation of a Transfer Climate Instrument." *Human Resource Development Quarterly, 8*(2), 95–113.

Hunt, V.D. (1996). *Process Mapping: How to Reengineer Your Business Processes.* New York: John Wiley & Sons.

Huws, U., S. Podro, E. Gunnarsson, T. Weijers, K. Arvanitaki, and V. Trova. (1996). "Teleworking and Gender." *Institute of Employment Studies, 317,* Grantham, UK: Grantham Book Services.

Jacobs, R.L., and M.J. Jones. (1995). *Structured On-the-Job Training: Unleashing Employee Expertise in the Workplace.* San Francisco: Berrett-Koehler Publishers.

Johann, B. (1995). *Designing Cross-Functional Business Processes.* San Francisco: Jossey-Bass.

Kaplan, R.S., and D.P. Norton. (1996). *The Balanced Scorecard: Translating Strategy into Action.* Boston: Harvard Business School.

Kaufman, R., and J.M. Keller. (1994). "Levels of Evaluation: Beyond Kirkpatrick." *Human Resource Development Quarterly, 5*(4), 371–380.

Kaufman, R., S. Thiagarajan, and P. MacGillis. (1997). *The Guidebook for Performance Improvement: Working with Individuals and Organizations.* San Francisco: Jossey-Bass.

Kemmerer, F.N., and S. Thiagarajan. (1992). "Incentive Systems." In *Handbook of Human Performance Technology: A Comprehensive Guide for Analyzing and Solving Performance Problems in Organizations,* H.D. Stolovitch & E.J. Keeps, editors. San Francisco: Jossey-Bass.

Kirkpatrick, D.L. (1998). *Evaluating Training Programs: The Four Levels.* San Francisco: Berrett-Koehler Publishers.

Kramlinger, T. (1998). "How to Deliver a Change Message." *Training & Development, 52*(4), 44–47.

Kuhnert, K., and D.P. McCauley. (1996). "Applying Alternative Survey Methods." In *Organizational Surveys: Tools for Assessment and Change,* A.I. Kraut, editor. San Francisco: Jossey-Bass.

Lawler, E.E. (1990). *Strategic Pay: Aligning Organizational Strategies and Pay Systems.* San Francisco: Jossey-Bass.

Lawler, E.E. (1998). "Strategic Pay System Design." In *Tomorrow's Organization: Crafting Winning Capabilities in a Dynamic World,* S.A. Mohrman, J.R. Galbraith & E. Lawler III, editors. San Francisco: Jossey-Bass.

Lawler, P.A. (1998). "The Ethics of Evaluating Training." In *Evaluating Corporate Training: Models and Issues,* S.M. Brown & C.J. Seidner, editors. Boston: Kluwer Academic Publishers.

Lipnack, J., and J. Stamps. (1998). *Virtual Teams: Reaching Across Space, Time, and Organizations with Technology.* New York: John Wiley & Sons.

McKenzie, R.B., and D.R. Lee. (1998). *Managing Through Incentives: How to Develop a More Collaborative, Productive, and Profitable Organization.* New York: Oxford University Press.

McLagan, P.A. (1997). "Competencies: The Next Generation." *Training & Development, 51*(5), 40–47.

Messmer, M. (1999). *Human Resources Kit for Dummies.* Foster City, CA: IDG Book Worldwide.

Mirabile, R.J. (1997). "Everything You Wanted to Know About Competency Modeling." *Training & Development, 51*(8), 73–77.

Newstrom, J.W., and M.L. Lengnick-Hall. (1991). "One Size Does Not Fit All." *Training & Development, 45*(6), 43–47.

Nilles, J.M. (1998). *Managing Telework: Strategies for Managing the Virtual Workplace.* New York: John Wiley & Sons.

Nolan, M. (1996). "Job Training." In *The ASTD Training & Development Handbook: A Guide to Human Resource Development* (4th edition), R.L. Craig, editor. New York: McGraw-Hill.

Nonaka, I., and H. Takeuchi. (1996). *The Knowledge Creating Company.* New York: Oxford University Press.

Parker, S., and T. Wall. (1998). *Job and Work Design: Organizing Work to Promote Well-Being and Effectiveness.* Thousand Oaks, CA: Sage Publications.

Parry, S.B. (1998). "Just What Is a Competency? And Why Should You Care?" *Training, 35*(6), 58–64.

Phillips, J.J. (1997). *Handbook of Training Evaluation and Measurement Methods* (3d edition). Houston, TX: Gulf Publishing Company.

Piskurich, G. (1997). "New Technologies for Telecommuters." *Training & Development, 51*(8), 78–79.

Reynolds, A. (1996). "Individualized Instructional Approaches." In *The ASTD Training & Development Handbook* (4th edition), R.L. Craig, editor. New York: McGraw-Hill.

Robinson, D.G., and J.C. Robinson. (1995). *Performance Consulting: Moving Beyond Training.* San Francisco: Berrett-Koehler Publishers.

Robinson, D.G., and J.C. Robinson, editors. (1998). *Moving from Training to Performance: A Practical Guidebook.* San Francisco: Berrett-Koehler Publishers.

Robinson, D.G., and J.C. Robinson. (1999). In *Handbook of Human Performance Technology: A Comprehensive Guide for Analyzing and Solving Performance Problems in Organizations* (2d edition), H.D. Stolovitch & E.J. Keeps, editors. San Francisco: Jossey-Bass.

Rosenberg, M.J. (1996). "Human Performance Technology." In *The ASTD Training & Development Handbook* (4th edition). R.L. Craig, editor. New York: McGraw-Hill.

Rossett, A. (1995). "Job Aids and EPSS." In *The ASTD Technical and Skills Training Handbook,* L. Kelly, editor. New York: McGraw-Hill.

Rossett, A., and J. Gautier-Downes. (1991). *A Handbook of Job Aids.* San Francisco: Pfeiffer.

Rouiller, J.Z., and I.L. Goldstein. (1993). "The Relationship Between Organizational Transfer Climate and Positive Transfer of Training." *Human Resource Development Quarterly, 4*(4), 377–390.

Rummler, G.A., and A.P. Brache. (1995). *Improving Performance: How to Manage the White Space on the Organizational Chart.* San Francisco: Jossey-Bass.

Scott, C.D., and D.T. Jaffe. (1989). *Managing Organizational Change: Becoming an Effective Change Agent.* Menlo Park, CA: Crisp Publications.

Shrock, S.A., and W.C. Coscarelli. (1989). *Criterion-Referenced Test Development: Technical and Legal Guidelines for Corporate Training.* Reading, MA: Addison-Wesley Publishing.

Spector, P.E. (1997). *Job Satisfaction: Application, Assessment, Causes, and Consequences.* Thousand Oaks, CA: Sage Publications.

Stewart, T.A. (1997). *Intellectual Capital: The New Wealth of Organizations.* New York: Doubleday.

Stolovitch, H.D., and E.J. Keeps, editors. (1992). *Handbook of Human Performance Technology: A Comprehensive Guide for Analyzing and Solving Performance Problems in Organizations.* San Francisco: Jossey-Bass.

Sugrue, B., and J. Fuller. (1999). *Performance Interventions: Selecting, Implementing, and Evaluating the Results.* Alexandria, VA: American Society for Training & Development.

Swanson, R.A. (1999). "Foundation of Performance Improvement and Implications for Practice." *Advances in Developing Human Resources, 1,* 1–25.

Tenner, A.R., and I.J. DeToro. (1997). *Process Redesign: The Implementation Guide for Managers.* Menlo Park, CA: Addison-Wesley Publishing.

Tesoro, F., and J. Tootson. (2000). *Implementing Global Performance Measurement Systems: A Cookbook Approach.* San Francisco: Jossey-Bass.

Torres, R.T., H.S. Preskill, and M.E. Piontek. (1996). *Evaluation Strategies for Communicating and Reporting: Enhancing Learning in Organizations.* Thousand Oaks, CA: Sage Publications.

Trochim, W. (1999). *The Research Methods Knowledge Base* (2d edition). Ithaca, NY: Cornell Custom Publishing.

Westgard, O. (1999). *Tests That Work: Designing and Delivering Fair and Practical Measurement Tools in the Workplace.* San Francisco: Jossey-Bass.

Wilson, T.B. (1994). *Innovative Reward Systems for a Changing Workplace.* New York: McGraw-Hill.

Youker, R.B. (1985). "Ten Benefits of Participant Action Planning." *Training, 22*(6), 52–56.

ADDITIONAL RESOURCES

Books

Austin, R.D. (1996). *Measuring and Managing Performance in Organizations.* New York: Dorset House.

Babbie, E. (1992). *The Practice of Social Research.* Belmont, CA: Wadsworth.

Barber, A.E. (1998). *Recruiting Employees: Individual and Organizational Perspectives.* Thousand Oaks, CA: Sage Publications.

Berger, L.A., and M.J. Sikora, editors. (1994). *The Change Management Handbook: A Roadmap to Corporate Transformation.* Chicago: Irwin Professional Publishing.

Block, P. (1981). *Flawless Consulting: A Guide for Getting Your Expertise Used.* San Diego: Pfeiffer & Company.

Botkin, J. (1999). *Smart Business: How Knowledge Communities Can Revolutionize Your Company.* New York: The Free Press.

Bowsher, J.E. (1998). *Revolutionizing Workplace Performance: A Systems Approach to Mastery.* San Francisco: Jossey-Bass.

Bray, D.W., editor. (1991). *Working with Organizations and Their People: A Guide to Human Resources Practice.* New York: The Guilford Press.

Brief, A.P. (1998). *Attitudes In and Around Organizations.* Thousand Oaks, CA: Sage Publications.

Brinkerhoff, R.O. (1995). "Using Evaluation to Improve the Quality of Technical Training." In *The ASTD Technical and Skills Training Handbook,* L. Kelly, editor. New York: McGraw-Hill.

Brinkerhoff, R.O. (1987). *Achieving Results from Training.* San Francisco: Jossey-Bass.

Brinkerhoff, R.O., and D.E. Dressler. (1990). *Productivity Measurement: A Guide for Managers and Evaluators.* Newbury Park, CA: Sage Publications.

Brown, S.M., and C.J. Seidner, editors. (1998). *Evaluating Corporate Training: Models and Issues.* Boston: Kluwer Academic Publishers.

Butteriss, M., editor. (1998). *Re-inventing HR: Changing Roles to Create the High-Performance Organization.* New York: John Wiley & Sons.

Campbell, D.T., and J.C. Stanley. (1963). *Experimental and Quasi-Experimental Designs for Research.* Dallas, TX: Houghton Mifflin Company.

Carmines, E.G., and R.A. Zeller. (1979). *Reliability and Validity Assessment.* Newbury Park, CA: Sage Publications.

Clardy, A. (1997). *Studying Your Workforce: Applied Research Methods and Tools for the Training and Development Practitioner.* Thousand Oaks, CA: Sage Publishers.

Conger, J.A., G.M. Spreitzer, and E.E. Lawler III, editors. (1998). *The Leader's Change Handbook: An Essential Guide to Setting Direction and Taking Action.* San Francisco: Jossey-Bass.

Cooper, C., and C. Argyris, editors. (1998). *The Concise Blackwell Encyclopedia of Management.* Malden, MS: Blackwell.

Czarnecki, M.T. (1999). *Managing by Measuring: How to Improve Your Organization's Performance Through Effective Benchmarking.* New York: AMACOM.

Daniels, W.R., and J.G. Mathers. (1997). *Change-able Organization: Key Management Practices for Speed and Flexibility.* Mill Valley, CA: ACT Publishing.

Davenport, T. (1999). *Human Capital: What it is and Why People Invest in It.* San Francisco: Jossey-Bass.

Dotlich, D.L., and J.L. Noel. (1998). *Action Learning: How the World's Top Companies Are Re-Creating Their Leaders and Themselves.* San Francisco: Jossey-Bass.

Dubois, D.D. (1993). *Competency-Based Performance Improvement: A Strategy for Organizational Change.* Amherst, MA: HRD Press.

Egan, G. (1994). *Working the Shadow Side: A Guide to Positive Behind-the-Scenes Management.* San Francisco: Jossey-Bass.

Emmons, S., and A. Thomas. (1998). *Transcending Performance Barriers.* Oxford, UK: Oxford University Press.

Esque, T.J. (1999). *No Surprises Project Management: A Proven Early Warning System for Staying on Track.* Mill Valley, CA: ACT Publishing.

Esque, T.J., and P.A. Patterson, editors. (1998). *Getting Results: Case Studies in Performance Improvement* (volume 1). Amherst, MA: HRD Press.

Falletta, S.V., and W.L. Combs. (1997, September). "Evaluating Technical Training: A Functional Approach." *Info-line,* 9709 (1-20).

Fink, A. (1995). *How to Analyze Survey Data: The Survey Kit* (volume 8). Newbury Park, CA: Sage Publications.

Fink, A. (1995). *How to Design Surveys: The Survey Kit* (volume 5). Newbury Park, CA: Sage Publications.

Fitz-enz, J. (1995). *How to Measure Human Resource Management* (2d edition). New York: McGraw-Hill.

Fletcher, J.L. (1993). *Patterns of High Performance: Discovering the Ways People Work Best.* San Francisco: Berrett-Koehler Publishers.

Folkman, J. (1998). *Employee Surveys That Make a Difference: Using Customized Feedback Tools to Transform Your Organization.* Provo, UT: Executive Excellence Publishing.

Fowler, F.J., and T.W. Mangione. (1990). *Standardized Survey Interviewing: Minimizing Interviewer-Related Error.* Thousand Oaks, CA: Sage Publications.

Friedman, B., J. Hatch, and D.M. Walker. (1998). *Delivering on the Promise: How to Attract, Manage, and Retain Human Capital.* New York: Free Press.

Fuller, J., and J. Farrington. (1999). *From Training to Performance Improvement: Navigating the Transition.* San Francisco: Pfeiffer.

Gilbert, T.F. (1996). *Human Competence: Engineering Worthy Performance* (tribute edition). New York: McGraw-Hill.

Giley, J.W., and N.W. Boughton. (1996). *Stop Managing, Start Coaching: How Performance Coaching Can Enhance Commitment and Improve Productivity.* New York: McGraw-Hill.

Gilley, J.W., and A.J. Coffern. (1994). *Internal Consulting for HRD Professionals: Tools, Techniques, and Strategies for Improving Organizational Performance.* Chicago: Irwin.

Green, P. (1999). *Building Robust Competencies: Linking Human Resource Systems to Organizational Strategies.* San Francisco: Jossey-Bass.

Greenberg, J., editor. (1994). *Organizational Behavior: The State of the Science.* Hillsdale, NJ: Lawrence Erlbaum Associates.

Grove, A. (1996). *Only the Paranoid Survive: How to Exploit the Crisis Points That Challenge Every Company.* New York: Doubleday.

Gubman, E.L. (1998). *The Talent Solution: Aligning Strategy and People to Achieve Extraordinary Results.* New York: McGraw-Hill.

Gupta, K. (1999). *A Practical Guide to Needs Assessment.* San Francisco: Pfeiffer.

Gutteridge, T.G., Z.B. Leibowitz, and J.E. Shore. (1993). *Organizational Career Development: Benchmarks for Building a World-Class Workforce.* San Francisco: Jossey-Bass.

Hackman, J.R., and G.R. Oldham. (1980). *Work Redesign.* Menlo Park, CA: Addison-Wesley Publishing.

Hale, J.A. (1998). *The Performance Consultant's Fieldbook: Tools and Techniques for Improving Organizations and People.* San Francisco: Pfeiffer.

Hannum, W., and C. Hansen. (1989). *Instructional Systems Development in Large Organizations.* Englewood Cliffs, NJ: Educational Technology Publications.

Harbour, J.L. (1997). *The Basics of Performance Measurement.* White Plains, NY: Quality Resources.

Harris, J., and J. Brannick. (1999). *Finding and Keeping Great Employees.* New York: AMACOM.

Harrison, M.I., and A. Shirom. (1999). *Organizational Diagnosis and Assessment: Bridging Theory and Practice.* Thousand Oaks, CA: Sage Publications.

Horibe, F. (1999). *Managing Knowledge Workers: New Skills and Attitudes to Unlock the Intellectual Capital in Your Organization.* New York: John Wiley & Sons.

Howard, A., editor. (1994). *Diagnosis for Organizational Change: Methods and Models.* New York: The Guilford Press.

Hunter, D., A. Bailey, and B. Taylor. (1995). *The Art of Facilitation: How to Create Group Synergy.* Tucson, AZ: Fisher Books.

Ilgen, D., and E. Pulakos, editors. (1999). *The Changing Nature of Performance: Implications for Staffing, Motivation, and Development.* San Francisco, CA: Jossey-Bass.

Jacobs, R.W. (1997). *Real Time Strategic Change.* San Francisco: Berrett-Koehler Publishers.

Jeanneret, R., and R. Silzer. (1998). *Individual Psychological Assessment: Predicting Behavior in Organizational Settings.* San Francisco: Jossey-Bass.

Joint Committee on Standards. (1994). *Program Evaluation Standards* (2d edition). Newbury Park, CA: Sage Publications.

Kane, M.B., and R. Mitchell, editors. (1996). *Implementing Performance Assessment: Promises, Problems, and Challenges.* Hillsdale, NJ: Lawrence Erlbaum Associates.

Kanji, G.K. (1993). *100 Statistical Tests.* Thousand Oaks, CA: Sage Publications.

Katzenbach, J.R., editor. (1995). *Real Change Leaders: How You Can Create Growth and High Performance in Your Company.* New York: Random House.

Kaye, B.L. (1997). *Up Is Not the Only Way: A Guide to Developing Workforce Talent* (2d edition). Palo Alto, CA: Davies-Black Publishing.

Knouse, S.B. (1995). *The Reward and Recognition Process in Total Quality Management.* Milwaukee, WI: ASQC Quality Press.

Kramer, R.M., and T.R. Tyler, editors. (1996). *Trust in Organizations: Frontiers of Theory and Research.* Thousand Oaks, CA: Sage Publications.

Kraut, A., and A. Korman, editors. (1999). *Evolving Practices in Human Resource Management: Responses to a Changing World of Work.* San Francisco: Jossey-Bass.

Langdon, D., K. Whiteside, and M. McKenna, editors. (1999). *Intervention Resource Guide: 50 Performance Improvement Tools.* San Francisco: Pfeiffer.

Lawler III, E.E. (2000). *Rewarding Excellence: Pay Strategies for the New Economy.* San Francisco: Jossey-Bass.

London, M., editor. (1995). *Employees, Careers, and Job Creation: Developing Growth-Oriented Human Resource Strategies and Programs.* San Francisco: Jossey-Bass.

Love, A.J. (1991). *Internal Evaluation: Building Organizations From Within.* Newbury Park, CA: Sage Publications.

Lyman, H.B. (1986). *Test Scores and What They Mean* (4th edition). Englewood Cliffs, NJ: Prentice-Hall.

MacDonald, J. (1998). *Calling a Halt to Mindless Change: A Plea for Commonsense Management.* New York: AMACOM.

Mager, R.F. (1975). *Preparing Instructional Objectives* (2d edition). Belmont, CA: Fearon Publishers.

Marks, M.L., and P.H. Mirvis. (1998). *Joining Forces: Making One Plus One Equal Three in Mergers, Acquisitions, and Alliances.* San Francisco: Jossey-Bass.

McCauley, C.D., R.S. Moxley, and E. Van Velsor. (1998). *The Center for Creative Leadership: Handbook of Leadership Development.* San Francisco: Jossey-Bass.

Mendelson, H., and J. Ziegler. (1999). *Survival of the Smartest: Managing Information for Rapid Action and World-Class Performance.* New York: John Wiley & Sons.

Meyer, J.P., and N.J. Allen. (1997). *Commitment in the Workplace: Theory, Research, and Application.* Thousand Oaks, CA: Sage Publications.

Mohrman, S.A., J.R. Galbraith, and E.E. Lawler III, editors. (1998). *Tomorrow's Organization: Crafting Winning Capabilities in a Dynamic World.* San Francisco: Jossey-Bass.

Morgan, G. (1998). *Images of Organization* (executive edition). San Francisco: Berrett-Koehler Publishers.

Newman, D.L., and R.D. Brown. (1996). *Applied Ethics for Program Evaluation.* Thousand Oaks, CA: Sage Publications.

Nicholson, N., editor. (1998). *The Blackwell Encyclopedic Dictionary of Organizational Behavior.* Malden, MS: Blackwell.

Nilson, C. (1999). *The Performance Consulting Toolkit: Tools and Activities for Trainers in a Performance Consulting Role.* New York: McGraw-Hill.

O'Driscoll, T. (1999). *Achieving Desired Business Performance: A Framework for Developing Human Performance Technology in Organizations.* Washington, DC: International Society for Performance Improvement.

Owen, J., and P.J. Rogers. (1999). *Program Evaluation: Forms and Approaches.* Thousand Oaks, CA: Sage Publications.

Pepitone, J.S. (1995). *Future Training: A Roadmap for Restructuring the Training Function.* Dallas, TX: AddVantage Learning Press.

Phillips, J.J., editor. (1998). *In Action: Implementing Evaluation Systems and Processes.* Alexandria, VA: American Society for Training & Development.

Preskill, H., and R.T. Torres. (1999). *Evaluative Inquiry for Learning in Organizations.* Thousand Oaks, CA: Sage.

Ravet, S., and M. Layte. (1997). *Technology-Based Training: A Comprehensive Guide to Choosing, Implementing, Managing, and Developing New Technologies in Training.* Houston, TX: Gulf Publishing.

Robbins, II., and M. Finley. (1996). *Why Change Doesn't Work: Why Initiatives Go Wrong and How to Try Again And Succeed.* Princeton, NJ: Pacesetter Books.

Rossett, A. (1999). *First Things Fast: A Handbook for Performance Analysis.* San Francisco: Pfeiffer.

Rothwell, W.J. (1996). *ASTD Models for Human Performance Improvement: Roles, Competencies, Outputs.* Alexandria, VA: American Society for Training & Development.

Rousseau, D.M. (1995). *Psychological Contracts in Organizations: Understanding Written and Unwritten Agreements.* Thousand Oaks, CA: Sage Publications.

Russ-Eft, D., H. Preskill, and C. Sleezer. (1997). *Human Resource Development Review: Research and Implications.* Newbury Park, CA: Sage Publications.

Schmitt, N., and R. Klimoski. (1991). *Research Methods in Human Resources Management.* Cincinnati, OH: South-Western Publishing.

Schreiber, D.A., and Z.L. Berge, editors. (1998). *Distance Training: How Innovative Organizations are Using Technology to Maximize Learning and Meet Business Objectives.* San Francisco: Jossey-Bass.

Scriven, M. (1991). *Evaluation Thesaurus* (4th edition). Newbury Park, CA: Sage Publications.

Shaffer, R.H. (1997). *High-Impact Consulting: How Clients and Consultants Can Leverage Rapid Results into Long-Term Gains.* San Francisco: Jossey-Bass.

Shandler, D. (1996). *Reengineering the Training Function: How to Align Training with the New Corporate Agenda.* Delray Beach, FL: St. Lucie Press.

Smart, B. (1999). *Topgrading: How Leading Companies Win by Hiring, Coaching, and Keeping the Best People.* Paramus, NJ: Prentice Hall Press.

Smither, J.W., editor. (1998). *Performance Appraisal: State of the Art in Practice.* San Francisco: Jossey-Bass.

Spencer, L.M., and S.M. Spencer. (1993). *Competence at Work: Models for Superior Performance.* New York: John Wiley & Sons.

Stewart, D.W., and P.N. Shamdasani. (1990). *Focus Groups: Theory and Practice.* Newbury Park, CA: Sage Publications.

Sudman, S., N. Bradburn, and N. Schwarz. (1996). *Thinking About Answers: The Application of Cognitive Processes to Survey Methodology.* San Francisco: Jossey-Bass.

Swanson, R.A. (1994). *Analysis for Improving Performance: Tools for Diagnosing Organizations & Documenting Workplace Expertise.* San Francisco: Berrett-Koehler Publishers.

Swanson, R.A., and E.F. Holton, editors. (1997). *Research Handbook: Linking Research and Practice.* San Francisco: Berrett-Koehler Publishers.

Swanson, R.A., and E.F. Holton. (1999). *Results: How to Assess Performance, Learning, and Perceptions.* San Francisco: Berrett-Koehler Publishers.

Tobin, D.R. (1998). *The Knowledge-Enabled Organization: Moving From "Training" to "Learning" to Meet Business Goals.* New York: AMACOM.

Tornow, W.W., and M. London, editors. (1998). *Maximizing the Value of 360-Degree Feedback: A Process for Successful Individual and Organizational Development.* San Francisco: Jossey-Bass.

Ulrich, D. (1997). *Human Resource Champions: The Next Agenda for Adding Value and Delivering Results.* Boston: Harvard Business School Press.

Ulrich, D., J. Zenger, and N. Smallwood. (1999). *Results-Based Leadership.* Boston: Harvard Business School Press.

Vaux, A., M.S. Stockdale, and M.J. Schwerin. (1992). *Independent Consulting for Evaluators.* Newbury Park, CA: Sage Publications.

Vella, J., P. Berardinelli, and J. Burrow. (1998). *How Do They Know They Know?: Evaluating Adult Learning.* San Francisco: Jossey-Bass.

Wallgren, A., B. Wallgren, R. Persson, U. Jorner, and J. Haaland. (1996). *Graphing Statistics and Data: Creating Better Charts.* Newbury Park, CA: Sage Publications.

Ward, M.E., and B. MacPhail-Wilcox. (1999). *Delegation and Empowerment: Leading with and Through Others.* Larchmont, NY: Eye on Education.

Weiss, T.B., and F. Hartle. (1997). *Reengineering Performance Management.* Boca Raton, FL: St. Lucie Press.

Wholey, J.S., H.P. Hatry, and K.E. Newcomer, editors. (1994). *Handbook of Practical Program Evaluation.* San Francisco: Jossey-Bass.

Witkin, B.R., and J.W. Altschuld. (1995). *Planning and Conducting Needs Assessments: A Practical Guide.* Newbury Park, CA: Sage Publications.

Articles

Alliger, G.M., S.I. Tannenbaum, W. Bennett, Jr., H. Traver, and A. Shotland. (1997). "A Meta-Analysis of the Relations Among Training Criteria." *Personnel Psychology, 50,* 341–358.

Atkinson, A.A., J.H. Waterhouse, and R.B. Wells. (1997, Spring). "A Stakeholder Approach to Strategic Performance Measurement." *Sloan Management Review,* 25–37.

Baldwin, T.T., and J.K. Ford. (1988). "Transfer of Training: A Review and Directions for Research." *Personnel Psychology, 41,* 63–105.

Berardinelli, P., J. Burrow, and L.D. Jones. (1995). "Management Training: An Impact Theory." *Human Resource Development Quarterly, 6*(1), 79–90.

Burke, W.W., and G.H. Litwin. (1992). "A Causal Model of Organizational Performance and Change." *Journal of Management, 18*(3), 523–545.

Cruz, B.J. (1997). "Measuring the Transfer of Training." *Performance Improvement Quarterly, 10*(2), 83–97.

DeMatteo, J.S., L.T. Eby, and E. Sundstrom. (1998). "Team-Based Rewards: Current Empirical Evidence and Directions for Future Research." *Research in Organizational Behavior, 20,* 141–183.

Dick, W., and D. King. (1994, October). "Formative Evaluation in the Performance Context." *Performance and Instruction,* 3–7.

Dixon, N.M. (1990). "The Relationship Between Trainee Responses on Participation Reaction Forms and Post-Test Scores." *Human Resource Development Quarterly, 1,* 129–137.

Duncan, W.J., P.M. Ginter, and L.E. Swayne. (1998). "Competitive Advantage and Internal Organizational Assessment." *Academy of Management Executive, 12*(3), 6–16.

Facteau, J.D., G.H. Dobbins, J.E. Russell, R.T. Ladd, and J.D. Kudisch. (1995). "The Influence of General Perceptions of the Training Environment in Pretraining Motivation and Perceived Training Transfer." *Journal of Management, 21*(1), 1–25.

Ford, J.K., and D.A. Weissbein. (1997). "Transfer of Training: Updated Review and Analysis." *Performance Improvement Quarterly, 10*(2), 22–41.

Forss, K., B. Cracknell, and K. Samset. (1994). "Can Evaluation Help an Organization to Learn?" *Evaluation Review, 18*(5), 574–591.

Guzzo, R.A., and M.W. Dickson. (1996). "Teams in Organizations: Recent Research on Performance and Effectiveness." *Annual Review of Psychology, 47,* 307–338.

Hale, J. (1988, February). "Evaluation: It's Time to Go Beyond Levels 1, 2, 3, and 4." *Performance Improvement, 37,* 30–34.

Johnson, S.T. (1993). "Work Teams: What's Ahead in Work Design and Rewards Management." *Compensation and Benefits Review, 25,* 35–41.

Kane, J.S., and K.A. Freeman. (1997). "A Theory of Equitable Performance Standards." *Journal of Management, 23*(1), 37–58.

Kanfer, R., and E.D. Heggestad. (1997). "Motivational Traits and Skills: A Person-Centered Approach to Work Motivation." *Research in Organizational Behavior, 19,* 1–56.

Kluger, A.N., and A. DeNisi. (1996). "The Effects of Feedback Interventions on Performance: A Historical Review, a Meta-Analysis, and a Preliminary Feedback Intervention Theory." *Psychological Bulletin, 119*(2), 254–284.

Kraiger, K., J.K. Ford, and E. Salas. (1993). "Application of Cognitive, Skill-Based, and Affective Theories of Learning Outcomes to New Methods of Training Evaluation." *Journal of Applied Psychology, 78*(2), 311–328.

Machin, M.A., and G.J. Fogarty. (1997). "The Effects of Self-Efficacy, Motivation to Transfer, and Situation Constraints on Transfer Intentions and Transfer of Training." *Performance Improvement Quarterly, 10*(2), 98–115.

McLinden, D., and W. Trochim. (1998, October). "Getting to Parallel: Assessing the Return on Expectations of Training." *Performance Improvement, 37,* 21–26.

Newstrom, J. (1995). "Review: Evaluating Training Programs: The Four Levels." *Human Resource Development Quarterly, 6*(3), 317–320.

Reichers, A.E., J.P. Wanous, and J.T. Austin. (1997). "Understanding and Managing Cynicism About Organizational Change." *Academy of Management Executives, 11*(1), 48–59.

Tannenbaum, S.I., and G. Yukl. (1992). "Training and Development in Work Organizations." *Annual Review of Psychology, 43,* 399–441.

Trochim, W.M. (1985). "Pattern Matching, Validity, and Conceptualization in Program Evaluation." *Evaluation Review, 9*(5), 575–604.

Waldman, D.A., L.E. Atwater, and D. Antonioni. (1998). "Has 360 Feedback Gone Amok?" *Academy of Management Executives, 12*(2), 86–94.

World Wide Web

Note: The online references are from the World Wide Web and include the appropriate URL address. Please keep in mind that in the future, some of these sites might move or be discontinued.

Academy of Human Resource Development Website (http://www.ahrd.org).

American Educational Research Association (AERA) Website (http://www.aera.net).

American Evaluation Association (AEA) Website (http://www.eval.org).

American Psychological Association (APA) Website (http://www.apa.org).

American Society for Training & Development (ASTD) Website (http://www.astd.org).

Conference Board Website (http://www.conference-board.org).

EPSS.com! Website (http://www.epss.com).

International Society for Performance Improvement (ISPI) Website (http://www.ispi.org).

Knowledge Management Magazine Website (http://www.kmmag.com).

Society for Applied Learning Technology (SALT) Website (http://www.salt.org).

Society for Human Resource Management Website (http://www.shrm.org).

Society for Industrial and Organizational Psychology Website (http://www.siop.org).

Trochim, William M. The Research Methods Knowledge Base, 2nd Edition. Website (http://trochim.human.cornell.edu/kb/index.htm).

ABOUT THE AUTHORS

Wendy L. Combs

Wendy is a program manager for Worldwide Training at Cisco Systems and manages the analysis, design, and development of e-learning initiatives. She has previously been involved in large-scale change initiatives: ERP systems implementation, process redesign, curriculum development, and performance improvement. She was formerly a training manager at Nortel Networks. Wendy has a doctoral degree in educational research and evaluation from North Carolina State University, a master's degree in psychology from Eastern Washington University, and a bachelor's degree in psychology from the University of California at Davis. Wendy was a school psychologist before moving into the field of adult learning. She has worked and consulted in schools, government, universities, and business, primarily in the role of data gathering for executive decision making. Wendy has expertise in designing and implementing organizational surveys, needs assessment, focus group methodology, and structured interviewing techniques. She is a member of the American Society for Training & Development, the International Society for Performance Improvement, and the American Psychological Association.

Salvatore V. Falletta

Sal is manager of the Global HR Research & Analysis group within Intel University—Learning and Development, a division of corporate human resources at Intel Corporation. He is responsible for Intel's global employee survey and organizational assessment strategy, measurement and evaluation initiatives, HR metrics and scorecard indicators, and applied people and organizational behavior research. Sal was formerly a training and organizational development manager, senior performance consultant, and senior evaluation consultant for two global telecommunications companies, Nortel Networks and Alltel. Sal earned a doctoral degree in training and development from North Carolina State University and a master's degree in public administration with a specialty in HR and OD from Indiana State University. He also holds a bachelor's degree in psychology from Eastern Washington University. His interests include assessment, measurement, evaluation, human performance improvement, organizational diagnosis, and strategic planning. Sal is a member of the American Society for Training & Development, the International Society for Performance Improvement, the Academy of Human Resource Development, the Society for Human Resource Management, the American Psychological Association, and the Society for Industrial and Organizational Psychology.